The Spirit of Discovery by William Lisle Bowles

William Lisle Bowles was born on 24th September 1762 at King's Sutton in Northamptonshire.

His great-grandfather, grandfather and his father, William Thomas Bowles, had all been parish priests and inevitably Bowles would join their line.

In 1789 Bowles published, a small quarto volume, Fourteen Sonnets, which was received with extraordinary praise, not only by the general public, but by such revered poets as Samuel Taylor Coleridge and Wordsworth.

After receiving his degree at Oxford, Bowles now began his career in service to the Church of England.

His years of service perhaps diminished both his stature as a poet and certainly the way he was viewed. For much of his career Bowles was seen as rather soft when set against his contemporaries but in the end his ability as a poet was enshrined, after a long and ferocious attack against him, by the principles he so eloquently wrote about and adhered too.

In personality and nature Bowles was said to be an amiable, absent-minded, but rather eccentric man. His poems speak warmly of a refinement of feeling, tenderness, and pensive thought, but are lacking in power and passion. But that should not diminish their value or appreciation to us.

Bowles maintained that images drawn from nature are poetically finer than those drawn from art; and that in the highest kinds of poetry the themes or passions handled should be of the general or elemental kind, and not the transient manners of any society.

As well as his poetry Bowles was also responsible for writing a Life of Bishop Ken (in two volumes, 1830–1831), Coombe Ellen and St. Michael's Mount (1798), The Battle of the Nile (1799), and The Sorrows of Switzerland (1801).

William Lisle Bowles died on April 7th, 1850 at the age of 87.

Index of Contents

THE SPIRIT OF DISCOVERY BY SEA

A DESCRIPTIVE AND HISTORICAL POEM

INTRODUCTION

I need not perhaps inform the reader, that I had before written a Canto on the subject of this poem; but I was dissatisfied with the metre, and felt the necessity of some connecting idea that might give it a degree of unity and coherence.

This difficulty I considered as almost inseparable from the subject; I therefore relinquished the design of making an extended poem on events, which, though highly interesting and poetical, were too unconnected with each other to unite properly in one regular whole. But on being kindly permitted to peruse the sheets of Mr Clarke's valuable work on the History of Navigation, I conceived (without supposing historically with him that all ideas of navigation were derived from the ark of Noah) that I might adopt the circumstance poetically, as capable of furnishing an unity of design; besides which, it had the advantage of giving a more serious cast and character to the whole.

To obviate such objections as might be made by those who, from an inattentive survey, might imagine there was any carelessness of arrangement, I shall lay before the reader a general analysis of the several books; and, I trust, he will readily perceive a leading principle, on which the poem begins, proceeds, and ends.

I feel almost a necessity for doing this in justice to myself, as some compositions have been certainly misunderstood, where the connexion might, by the least attention, have been perceived. In going over part of the same ground which I had taken before, I could not always avoid the use of similar expressions.

I trust I need not apologise for having, in some instances, departed from strict historical facts. It is not true that Camoens sailed with De Gama, though, from the authority of Voltaire, it has been sometimes supposed that he did. There are other circumstances for which I may have less reason to expect pardon. The Egyptians were never, or but for a short time, a maritime nation. In answer to this, I must say, that history and poetry are two things; and though the poet has no right to contradict the historian, yet, if he find two opinions upon points of history, he may certainly take that which is most susceptible of poetical ornament; particularly if it have sufficient plausibility, and the sanction of respectable names.

In deducing the first maritime attempts from Thebes, so called from Thebaoth, the Ark, founded by the sons of Cush, who first inhabited the caves on the granite mountains of Ethiopia, I have followed the idea of Bruce, which has many testimonies, particularly that of Herodotus, in its favour. In making the ships of Ammon first pass the straits of Babelmandel, and sail to Ophir, I have the authority of Sir Isaac Newton. But still these points must, from their nature, be obscure; the poet, however, has a right to build upon them, whilst what he advances is not in direct contradiction to all historical admitted facts. He may take what is shadowy, if it be plausible, poetical, and coherent with his general plan. Having said ingenuously thus much, I hope I shall not be severely accused for having admitted, en passant, some ideas (which may be thought visionary) in the notes, respecting the allusion to the ark in Theocritus, the situation of Ophir, the temple of Solomon, and the algum-tree.

I must also submit to the candour of the critic, the necessity I sometimes felt myself under of varying the verse, and admitting, when the subject seemed particularly to require it, a break into the measure. He will consider, as this poem is neither didactic, nor epic, that might lead on the mind by diversity of characters, and of prospects; it was therefore necessary (at least I thought myself at liberty so to do) to break the uniformity of the subject by digression, contrast, occasional change of verse, et cet. But after all, at a time so unfavourable to long poems, I doubt whether the reader will have patience to accompany me to the end of my circumnavigation. If he do, and if this much larger poetical work than I have ever attempted should be as favourably received as what I have before published has been, I shall sincerely rejoice.

At all events, in an age which I think has produced genuine poetry, if I cannot say "Ed Io, anchi, sono pittore;" it will be a consolation to me to reflect, that I have no otherwise courted the muse, than as the consoler of sorrow, the painter of scenes romantic and interesting, the handmaid of good sense, unadulterated feelings, and religious hope.

It was at first intended that the poem should consist of six books; one book being assigned to De Gama, and another to Columbus. These have been compressed. I was the more inclined to this course, as the great subject of the DISCOVERY OF AMERICA is in the hands of such poets as Mr Southey and Mr Rogers.

DONHEAD, Nov

Dedicated to His Royal Highness George Prince of Wales (afterwards George IV)

ANALYSIS

BOOK THE FIRST

The book opens with the resting of the Ark on the mountains of the great Indian Caucasus, considered by many authors as Ararat: the present state of the inhabited world, contrasted with its melancholy appearance immediately after the flood. The poem returns to the situation of our forefathers on leaving the ark; beautiful evening described. The Angel of Destruction appears to Noah in a dream, and informs him that although he and his family alone have escaped, the VERY ARK, which was the means of his present preservation, shall be the cause of the future triumph of Destruction.

In his dream, the evils in consequence of the discovery of America, the slave-trade, et cet., are set before him. Noah, waking from disturbed sleep, ascends the summit of Caucasus. An angel appears to him; tells him that the revelations in his dream were PERMITTED BY THE ALMIGHTY; that he is commissioned to explain everything; he presents to his view the shadow of the world as it exists; regions are pointed out; the dispersion of mankind; the rise of superstition; the birth of a SAVIOUR, and the triumph of Charity: that navigation shall be the means of extending the knowledge of GOD over the globe; and though some evils must take place, happiness and love shall finally prevail upon the earth.

BOOK THE SECOND

Commences with an ardent wish, that as our forefather viewed the world clearly displayed before him in a vision, so we of these late days might be able, through the clouds of time, to look back upon the early ages of the globe; we might then see, in their splendour, Thebes, Edom, et cet.; but the early history of mankind is obscure, the only certain light is from the sacred writings. By these we are informed of the dispersion of earth's first inhabitants, after the flood. The descendants of HAM, after this dispersion, according to Bruce, having first gained the summits of the Ethiopian mountains, there form subterraneous abodes. In process of time they descend, people Egypt, build Thebes; obscure tradition of the Ark; first make voyages.

Ophir is not long afterwards discovered. This Bruce places, on most respectable authority, at Sofala; I have ventured to place it otherwhere, but still admitting one general idea, that when the way to it overland was attended with difficulties, an easier course was at last opened by sea. As to Ammon's exploits, I must shelter myself under the authority of Sir Isaac Newton. After a sacrifice by the Egyptians, the monsoon sets in. The ships follow its direction, as the mariners imagine a god leads them. Hence the discovery of so much of the world by sea. Reflection on commerce. The voyage of Solomon. A description of the glory of TYRE, the most commercial mart of the early world. Tyrian discoveries in the Mediterranean; voyages to the coast of Italy and Spain, to the Straits, and from thence to Britain.

Tyre is destroyed, and the thought naturally arises, that Britain, which, at the time of the splendour of the maritime Tyrians, was an obscure island, is now at the summit of maritime renown; while TYRE is a place where only "the fisherman dries his net." This leads to an EULOGIUM ON ENGLAND; and the book concludes with the triumphs of her fleets and armies on that very shore, on which science, and art, and commerce, and MARITIME RENOWN, first arose.

This digression, introducing the siege of Acre, appeared to the author not only natural, but in some measure necessary to break the uniformity of the subject.

BOOK THE THIRD

Commences with the feelings excited by the conclusion of the last, by a warm wish that England may for ages retain her present elevated rank. This leads to the consideration of her NAVAL OPULENCE, which carries us back to the subject we had left—THE FATE OF TYRE.

The history of the empires succeeding Tyre is touched on: the fall of her destroyer, Babylon; the succession of Cyrus; the character of Cyrus, and his want of enlarged policy, having so many means of encouraging commerce; and his ill-fated expedition to the East Indies.

ALEXANDER THE GREAT first conceives the idea of establishing a vast MARITIME EMPIRE: in his march of conquest, he proceeds to the last river of the Punjab, the Hyphasis, which descends into the Indus, the sources of which are near the mountains of CAUCASUS, WHERE THE ARK RESTED.

The Indian account of the Deluge, it is well known, resembles most wonderfully the history of Moses. When Alexander can proceed no further, poetical fiction introduces the person of a Brahmin, who relates the history of the Deluge: viz., that one sacred man was, in this part of the world, miraculously preserved by an ark; the further march of the conqueror towards the holy spot is deprecated: his best glory shall be derived from the sea, and from uniting either world in commerce. Alexander is animated with the idea; and his fleet, under Nearchus, proceeds down the Indus to the sea. This forms a middle, connected with the account of the Deluge, book first.

BOOK THE FOURTH

Nearchus' voyage being accomplished, and Alexandria now complete, Commerce is represented as standing on the Pharos, and calling to all nations. The tide of commerce would have flowed still in the track pointed out by the sagacity of Alexander, but that a wider scene, beyond THE ANCIENT WORLD, opens to the VIEW OF DISCOVERY. The use of the magnet is discovered; and Henry of Portugal prosecutes the plan of opening a passage along the coast of Africa to the East. One of his ships on its return from the expedition has been driven from Cape Bojador (the formidable boundary of Portuguese research) by a storm at sea. The isle afterwards called Porto Santo is discovered. The circumstance related; but the extraordinary appearance of a supernatural shade over the waters at a distance excites many fears and superstitions. The attempt, however, to penetrate the mystery, is resolved on. Zarco reaches the island of Madeira; tomb found; which introduces the episode. At the tomb of the first discoverer (whether this be fanciful or not, is nothing to poetry) the Spirit of Discovery casts her eyes over the globe; she pursues De Gama to the East; history of Camoens touched on; Columbus; sees with triumph the discovery of a new world, and from thence extends her ideas till the great globe is encompassed; after which she returns to the "tranquil bosom of the Thames," with Drake, the first circumnavigator, whose ship, after its various perils, being laid up in that river, gives rise to some brief concluding reflections.

BOOK THE FIFTH

Hitherto we have described only the triumphs of Discovery; but it appears necessary that many incidental evils, special and general, should be mentioned. Fate and miserable end of some great commanders,—of our gallant and benevolent countryman, Cook. After the natural feelings of regret, the mind is led to contemplate the great advantages of his voyages: the health of seamen; the accessions to geographical knowledge; the spirit of humanity and science; his exploring the east part of New-Holland; and being the first to determine the proximity of America to Asia. This circumstance leads us back from the point whence we set out—THE ARK OF NOAH; and hence we are partly enabled to solve, what has been for so many ages unknown, the difficulty{g} respecting the earth's being peopled from one family.

The poem having thus gained a middle and end, the conclusion of the whole is, that as this uncertainty in the physical world has been by DISCOVERY cleared up, so all the apparent contradictions in the moral world shall be reconciled. We have yet many existing evils to deplore; but when the SUPREME DISPOSER's plan shall have been completed, then the earth, which has been explored and enlightened by discovery and knowledge, shall be destroyed; but the MIND OF MAN, rendered at last perfect, shall endure through all ages, and "justify His ways from whom it sprung."

Such is the outline and plan of the following poem. I have felt myself obliged to give this hasty analysis, thinking that self-defence almost required it, lest a careless reader might charge me with carelessness of arrangement.

I must again beg it to be remembered, that History and Poetry are two things; and that the poet has a right to build his system, not on what is exact truth, but on what is, at least, plausible; what will form, in the clearest manner, a WHOLE; and what is most susceptible of poetical ornament.

THE SPIRIT OF DISCOVERY BY SEA

BOOK THE FIRST

Awake a louder and a loftier strain!
Beloved harp, whose tones have oft beguiled
My solitary sorrows, when I left
The scene of happier hours, and wandered far,
A pale and drooping stranger; I have sat
(While evening listened to the convent bell)
On the wild margin of the Rhine, and wooed
Thy sympathies, "a-weary of the world,"
And I have found with thee sad fellowship,
Yet always sweet, whene'er my languid hand
Passed carelessly o'er the responsive wires,
While unambitious of the laurelled meed
That crowns the gifted bard, I only asked
Some stealing melodies, the heart might love,
And a brief sonnet to beguile my tears!

But I had hope that one day I might wake
Thy strings to loftier utterance; and now,
Bidding adieu to glens, and woods, and streams,
And turning where, magnificent and vast,
Main Ocean bursts upon my sight, I strike,—
Rapt in the theme on which I long have mused,—
Strike the loud lyre, and as the blue waves rock,
Swell to their solemn roar the deepening chords.

Lift thy indignant billows high, proclaim
Thy terrors, Spirit of the hoary seas!
I sing thy dread dominion, amid wrecks,
And storms, and howling solitudes, to Man
Submitted: awful shade of Camoens
Bend from the clouds of heaven.

By the bold tones
Of minstrelsy, that o'er the unknown surge
(Where never daring sail before was spread)
Echoed, and startled from his long repose
The indignant Phantom of the stormy Cape;

Oh, let me think that in the winds I hear
Thy animating tones, whilst I pursue
With ardent hopes, like thee, my venturous way,
And bid the seas resound my song! And thou,
Father of Albion's streams, majestic Thames,
Amid the glittering scene, whose long-drawn wave
Goes noiseless, yet with conscious pride, beneath
The thronging vessels' shadows; nor through scenes
More fair, the yellow Tagus, or the Nile,
That ancient river, winds. THOU to the strain
Shalt haply listen, that records the MIGHT
Of OCEAN, like a giant at thy feet
Vanquished, and yielding to thy gentle state
The ancient sceptre of his dread domain!

All was one waste of waves, that buried deep
Earth and its multitudes: the Ark alone,
High on the cloudy van of Ararat,
Rested; for now the death-commissioned storm
Sinks silent, and the eye of day looks out
Dim through the haze; while short successive gleams
Flit o'er the weltering Deluge as it shrinks,
Or the transparent rain-drops, falling few,
Distinct and larger glisten. So the Ark
Rests upon Ararat; but nought around
Its inmates can behold, save o'er th' expanse
Of boundless waters, the sun's orient orb
Stretching the hull's long shadow, or the moon
In silence, through the silver-cinctured clouds,
Sailing as she herself were lost, and left
In Nature's loneliness!

But oh, sweet Hope,
Thou bid'st a tear of holy ecstasy
Start to their eye-lids, when at night the Dove,
Weary, returns, and lo! an olive leaf
Wet in her bill: again she is put forth,
When the seventh morn shines on the hoar abyss:—
Due evening comes: her wings are heard no more!
The dawn awakes, not cold and dripping sad,
But cheered with lovelier sunshine; far away
The dark-red mountains slow their naked peaks
Upheave above the waste; Imaus gleams;
Fume the huge torrents on his desert sides;
Till at the awful voice of Him who rules
The storm, the ancient Father and his train
On the dry land descend.

Here let us pause.
No noise in the vast circuit of the globe
Is heard; no sound of human stirring: none
Of pasturing herds, or wandering flocks; nor song
Of birds that solace the forsaken woods
From morn till eve; save in that spot that holds
The sacred Ark: there the glad sounds ascend,
And Nature listens to the breath of Life.
The fleet horse bounds, high-neighing to the wind
That lifts his streaming mane; the heifer lows;
Loud sings the lark amid the rainbow's hues;
The lion lifts him muttering; MAN comes forth—
He kneels upon the earth—he kisses it;
And to the GOD who stretched that radiant bow,
He lifts his trembling transports.

From one spot
Alone of earth such sounds ascend. How changed
The human prospect! when from realm to realm,
From shore to shore, from isle to furthest isle,
Flung to the stormy main, man's murmuring race,
Various and countless as the shells that strew
The ocean's winding marge, are spread; from shores
Sinensian, where the passing proas gleam
Innumerous 'mid the floating villages:
To Acapulco west, where laden deep
With gold and gems rolls the superb galleon,
Shadowing the hoar Pacific: from the North,
Where on some snowy promontory's height
The Lapland wizard beats his drum, and calls
The spirits of the winds, to th' utmost South,
Where savage Fuego shoots its cold white peaks,
Dreariest of lands, and the poor Pecherais
Shiver and moan along its waste of snows.
So stirs the earth; and for the Ark that passed
Alone and darkling o'er the dread abyss,
Ten thousand and ten thousand barks are seen
Fervent and glancing on the friths and sounds;
From the Bermudian that, with masts inclined,
Shoots like a dart along; to the tall ship
That, like a stately swan, in conscious pride
Breasts beautiful the rising surge, and throws
The gathered waters back, and seems to move
A living thing, along her lucid way
Streaming in white-winged glory to the sun!
Some waft the treasures of the east; some bear
Their country's dark artillery o'er the surge
Frowning; some in the southern solitudes,

Bound on discovery of new regions, spread,
'Mid rocks of driving ice, that crash around,
Their weather-beaten mainsail; or explore
Their perilous way from isle to isle, and wind
The tender social tie; connecting man,
Wherever scattered, with his fellow-man.

How many ages rolled away ere thus,
From NATURE'S GENERAL WRECK, the world's great scene
Was tenanted! See from their sad abode,
At Heaven's dread voice, heard from the solitude,
As in the dayspring of created things,
The sad survivors of a buried world
Come forth; on them, though desolate their seat,
The sky looks down with smiles; for the broad sun,
That to the west slopes his untired career,
Hangs o'er the water's brim. The aged sire,
Now rising from his evening sacrifice,
Amid his offspring stands, and lifts his eyes,
Moist with a tear, to the bright bow: the fire
Yet on the altar burns, whose trailing fume
Goes slowly up, and marks the lucid cope
Of the soft sky, where distant clouds hang still
And beautiful. So placid Evening steals
After the lurid storm, like a sweet form
Of fairy following a perturbed shape
Of giant terror, that in darkness strode.
Slow sinks the lord of day; the clustering clouds
More ardent burn; confusion of rich hues,
Crimson, and gold, and purple, bright, inlay
Their varied edges; till before the eye,
As their last lustre fades, small silver stars
Succeed; and twinkling each in its own sphere,
Thick as the frost's unnumbered spangles, strew
The slowly-paling heavens. Tired Nature seems
Like one who, struggling long for life, had beat
The billows, and scarce gained a desert crag,
O'er-spent, to sink to rest: the tranquil airs
Whisper repose. Now sunk in sleep reclines
The Father of the world; then the sole moon
Mounts high in shadowy beauty; every cloud
Retires, as in the blue space she moves on
Amid the fulgent orbs supreme, and looks
The queen of heaven and earth. Stilly the streams
Retiring sound; midnight's high hollow vault
Faint echoes; stilly sound the distant streams.

When, hark! a strange and mingled wail, and cries

As of ten thousand thousand perishing!
A phantom, 'mid the shadows of the dead,
Before the holy Patriarch, as he slept,
Stood terrible:—Dark as a storm it stood
Of thunder and of winds, like hollow seas
Remote; meantime a voice was heard: Behold,
Noah, the foe of thy weak race! my name
Destruction, whom thy sons in yonder plains
Shall worship, and all grim, with mooned horns
Paint fabling: when the flood from off the earth
Before it swept the living multitudes,
I rode amid the hurricane; I heard
The universal shriek of all that lived.
In vain they climbed the rocky heights: I struck
The adamantine mountains, and like dust
They crumbled in the billowy foam. My hall,
Deep in the centre of the seas, received
The victims as they sank! Then, with dark joy,
I sat amid ten thousand carcases,
That weltered at my feet! But THOU and THINE
Have braved my utmost fury: what remains
But vengeance, vengeance on thy hated race;—
And be that sheltering shrine the instrument!
Thence, taught to stem the wild sea when it roars,
In after-times to lands remote, where roamed
The naked man and his wan progeny,
They, more instructed in the fatal use
Of arts and arms, shall ply their way; and thou
Wouldst bid the great deep cover thee to see
The sorrows of thy miserable sons:
But turn, and view in part the truths I speak.

He said, and vanished with a dismal sound
Of lamentation from his grisly troop.

Then saw the just man in his dream what seemed
A new and savage land: huge forests stretched
Their world of wood, shading like night the banks
Of torrent-foaming rivers, many a league
Wandering and lost in solitudes; green isles
Here shone, and scattered huts beneath the shade
Of branching palms were seen; whilst in the sun
A naked infant playing, stretched his hand
To reach a speckled snake, that through the leaves
Oft darted, or its shining volumes rolled
Erratic.

From the woods a sable man

Came, as from hunting; in his arms he took
The smiling child, that with the feathers played
Which nodded on his brow; the sheltering hut
Received them, and the cheerful smoke went up
Above the silent woods.

Anon was heard
The sound as of strange thunder, from the mouths
Of hollow engines, as, with white sails spread,
Tall vessels, hulled like the great Ark, approached
The verdant shores: they, in a woody cove
Safe-stationed, hang their pennants motionless
Beneath the palms. Meantime, with shouts and song,
The boat rows hurrying to the land; nor long
Ere the great sea for many a league is tinged,
While corpse on corpse, down the red torrent rolled,
Floats, and the inmost forests murmur—Blood.

Now vast savannahs meet the view, where high
Above the arid grass the serpent lifts
His tawny crest:—Not far a vessel rides
Upon the sunny main, and to the shore
Black savage tribes a mournful captive urge,
Who looks to heaven with anguish. Him they cast
Bound in the rank hold of the prison-ship,
With many a sad associate in despair,
Each panting chained to his allotted space;
And moaning, whilst their wasted eye-balls roll.

Another scene appears: the naked slave
Writhes to the bloody lash; but more to view
Nature forbad, for starting from his dream
The just Man woke. Shuddering he gazed around;
He saw the earliest beam of morning shine
Slant on the hills without; he heard the breath
Of placid kine, but troubled thoughts and sad
Arose. He wandered forth; and now far on,
By heavy musings led, reached a ravine
Most mild amid the tempest-riven rocks,
Through whose dark pass he saw the flood remote
Gray-spreading, while the mists of morn went up.
He paused; when on his lonely pathway flashed
A light, and sounds as of approaching wings
Instant were heard. A radiant form appeared,
Celestial, and with heavenly accent said:
Noah, I come commissioned from above,
Where angels move before th' eternal throne
Of heaven's great King in glory, to dispel

The mists of darkness from thy sight; for know,
Not unpermitted of th' Eternal One
The shadows of thy melancholy dream
Hung o'er thee slumbering: Mine the task to show
Futurity's faint scene;—now follow me.

He said; and up to the unclouded height
Of that great Eastern mountain, that surveys
Dim Asia, they ascended. Then his brow
The Angel touched, and cleared with whispered charm
The mortal mist before his eyes.—At once
(As in the skiey mirage, when the seer
From lonely Kilda's western summit sees
A wondrous scene in shadowy vision rise)
The NETHER WORLD, with seas and shores, appeared
Submitted to his view: but not as then,
A melancholy waste, deform and sad;
But fair as now the green earth spreads, with woods,
Champaign, and hills, and many winding streams
Robed, the magnificent illusion rose.
He saw in mazy longitude devolved
The mighty Brahma-Pooter; to the East
Thibet and China, and the shining sea
That sweeps the inlets of Japan, and winds
Amid the Curile and Aleutian isles,
Pale to the north. Siberia's snowy scenes
Are spread; Jenisca and the freezing Ob
Appear, and many a forest's shady track
Far as the Baltic, and the utmost bounds
Of Scandinavia; thence the eye returns:
And lo! great Lebanon—abrupt and dark
With pines, and airy Carmel, rising slow
Above the midland main, where hang the capes
Of Italy and Greece; swart Africa,
Beneath the parching sun, her long domain
Reveals, the mountains of the Moon, the source
Of Nile, the wild mysterious Niger, lost
Amid the torrid sands; and to the south
Her stormy cape. Beyond the misty main
The weary eye scarce wanders, when behold
Plata, through vaster territory poured;
And Andes, sweeping the horizon's tract,
Mightiest of mountains! whose eternal snows
Feel not the nearer sun; whose umbrage chills
The murmuring ocean; whose volcanic fires
A thousand nations view, hung like the moon
High in the middle waste of heaven; thy range,
Shading far off the Southern hemisphere,

A dusky file Titanic.

So spread
Before our great forefather's view the globe
Appeared; with seas, and shady continents,
And verdant isles, and mountains lifting dark
Their forests, and indenting rivers, poured
In silvery maze. And, Lo! the Angel said,
These scenes, O Noah, thy posterity
Shall people; but remote and scattered wide,
They shall forget their GOD, and see no trace,
Save dimly, of their Great Original.
Rude caves shall be their dwellings: till, with noise
Of multitudes, imperial cities rise.
But the Arch Fiend, the foe of GOD and man,
Shall fling his spells; and, 'mid illusions drear,
Blear Superstition shall arise, the earth
Eclipsing.—Deep in caves, vault within vault
Far winding; or in night of thickest woods,
Where no bird sings; or 'mid huge circles gray
Of uncouth stone, her aspect wild, and pale
As the terrific flame that near her burns,
She her mysterious rites, 'mid hymns and cries,
Shall wake, and to her shapeless idols, vast
And smeared with blood, or shrines of lust, shall lead
Her votaries, maddening as she waves her torch,
With visage more expanded, to the groans
Of human sacrifice.

Nor think that love
And happiness shall dwell in vales remote:
The naked man shall see the glorious sun,
And think it but enlightens his poor isle,
Hid in the watery waste; cold on his limbs
The ocean-spray shall beat; his Deities
Shall be the stars, the thunder, and the winds;
And if a stranger on his rugged shores
Be cast, his offered blood shall stain the strand.
O wretched man! who then shall raise thee up
From this thy dark estate, forlorn and lost?
The Patriarch said.

The Angel answered mild,
His God, who destined him to noblest ends!
But mutual intercourse shall stir at first
The sunk and grovelling spirit, and from sleep
The sullen energies of man rouse up,
As of a slumbering giant. He shall walk

Sublime amid the works of GOD: the earth
Shall own his wide dominion; the great sea
Shall toss in vain its roaring waves; his eye
Shall scan the bright orbs as they roll above
Glorious, and his expanding heart shall burn,
As wide and wider in magnificence
The vast scene opens; in the winds and clouds,
The seas, and circling planets, he shall see
The shadow of a dread Almighty move.
Then shall the Dayspring rise, before whose beam
The darkness of the world is past:—For, hark!
Seraphs and angel-choirs with symphonies
Acclaiming of ten thousand golden harps,
Amid the bursting clouds of heaven revealed,
At once, in glory jubilant, they sing—
God the Redeemer liveth! He who took
Man's nature on him, and in human shroud
Veiled his immortal glory! He is risen!
God the Redeemer liveth! And behold!
The gates of life and immortality
Open to all that breathe!

Oh, might the strains
But win the world to love; meek Charity
Should lift her looks and smile; and with faint voice
The weary pilgrim of the earth exclaim,
As close his eye-lids—Death, where is thy sting?
O Grave, where is thy victory?

And ye,
Whom ocean's melancholy wastes divide,
Who slumber to the sullen surge, awake,
Break forth into thanksgiving, for the bark
That rolled upon the desert deep, shall bear
The tidings of great joy to all that live,
Tidings of life and light.

Oh, were those men,
(The Patriarch raised his drooping looks, and said)
Such in my dream I saw, who to the isles
And peaceful sylvan scenes o'er the wide seas
Came tilting; then their murderous instruments
Lifted, that flashed to the indignant sun,
Whilst the poor native died:—Oh, were those men
Instructed in the laws of holier love,
Thou hast displayed?

The Angel meek replied—

Call rather fiends of hell those who abuse
The mercies they receive: that such, indeed,
On whom the light of clearer knowledge beams,
Should wander forth, and for the tender voice
Of charity should scatter crimes and woe,
And drench, where'er they pass, the earth with blood,
Might make ev'n angels weep:

But the poor tribes
That groaned and died, deem not them innocent
As injured; more ensanguined rites and deeds
Of deepest stain were theirs; and what if God,
So to approve his justice, and exact
Most even retribution, blood for blood,
Bid forth the Angel of the storm of death!

Thou saw'st, indeed, the seeming innocence
Of man the savage; but thou saw'st not all.
Behold the scene more near! hear the shrill whoop
Of murderous war! See tribes on neighbour tribes
Rush howling, their red hatchets wielding high,
And shouting to their barbarous gods! Behold
The captive bound, yet vaunting direst hate,
And mocking his tormentors, while they gash
His flesh unshrinking, tear his eyeballs, burn
His beating breast! Hear the dark temples ring
To groans and hymns of murderous sacrifice;
While the stern priest, the rites of horror done,
With hollow-echoing chaunt lifts up the heart
Of the last victim 'mid the yelling throng,
Quivering, and red, and reeking to the sun!
Reclaimed by gradual intercourse, his heart
Warmed with new sympathies, the forest-chief
Shall cast the bleeding hatchet to his gods
Of darkness, and one Lord of all adore—
Maker of heaven and earth.

Let it suffice,
He hath permitted EVIL for a while
To mingle its deep hues and sable shades
Amid life's fair perspective, as thou saw'st
Of late the blackening clouds; but in the end
All these shall roll away, and evening still
Come smilingly, while the great sun looks down
On the illumined scene. So Charity
Shall smile on all the earth, and Nature's God
Look down upon his works; and while far off
The shrieking night-fiends fly, one voice shall rise

From shore to shore, from isle to furthest isle—
Glory to God on high, and on earth peace,
Peace and good-will to men!

Thou rest in hope,
And Him with meekness and with trust adore!
He said, and spreading bright his ampler wing,
Flew to the heaven of heavens; the meek man bowed
Adoring, and, with pensive thoughts resigned,
Bent from the aching height his lonely way.

NOTES

See Camoens' description of the dreadful Phantom at the Cape of Good Hope.

Part of the mountainous range of the vast Indian Caucasus, where the Ark rested.

Forster says the miserable creatures who visited the ship in the Straits of Magellan, seldom uttered any other word than "Passeray"—hence the name of Pecherais was given to them.

From Dariena to Nicaragua, the Spaniards slew , people with dogs, sword, fire, and divers tortures.—Purchas.

That tremendous Caff (according to the Indian superstition) inhabited by spirits, demons, and the griffin Simorg.

The caves of Elephanta and Salsette.

At the dedication of the temple of Vitzuliputzli, A.D. ,human victims were sacrificed in four days.

BOOK THE SECOND

Oh for a view, as from that cloudless height
Where the great Patriarch gazed upon the world,
His offspring's future seat, back on the vale
Of years departed! We might then behold
Thebes, from her sleep of ages, awful rise,
Like an imperial shadow, from the Nile,
To airy harpings; and with lifted torch
Scatter the darkness through the labyrinths
Of death, where rest her kings, without a name,
And light the winding caves and pyramids
In the long night of years! We might behold
Edom, in towery strength, majestic rise,
And awe the Erithræan, to the plains

Where Migdol frowned, and Baal-zephon stood,
Before whose naval shrine the Memphian host
And Pharaoh's pomp were shattered! As her fleets
From Ezion went seaward, to the sound
Of shouts and brazen trumpets, we might say,
How glorious, Edom, in thy ships art thou,
And mighty as the rushing winds!

But night
Is on the mournful scene: a voice is heard,
As of the dead, from hollow sepulchres,
And echoing caverns of the Nile—So pass
The shades of mortal glory! One pure ray
From Sinai bursts (where God of old revealed
His glory, through the darkness terrible
That sat on the dread Mount), and we descry
Thy sons, O Noah! peopling wide the scene,
From Shinar's plain to Egypt.

Let the song
Reveal, who first "went down to the great sea
In ships," and braved the stormy element.

THE SONS OF CUSH. Still fearful of the FLOOD,
They on the marble range and cloudy heights
Of that vast mountain barrier,—which uprises
High o'er the Red Sea coast, and stretches on
With the sea-line of Afric's southern bounds
To Sofala,—delved in the granite mass
Their dark abode, spreading from rock to rock
Their subterranean cities, whilst they heard,
Secure, the rains of vexed Orion rush.
Emboldened they descend, and now their fanes
On Egypt's champaign darken, whilst the noise
Of caravans is heard, and pyramids
In the pale distance gleam. Imperial THEBES
Starts, like a giant, from the dust; as when
Some dread enchanter waves his wand, and towers
And palaces far in the sandy wilds
Spring up: and still, her sphinxes, huge and high,
Her marble wrecks colossal, seem to speak
The work of some great arm invisible,
Surpassing human strength; while toiling Time,
That sways his desolating scythe so vast,
And weary havoc murmuring at his side,
Smite them in vain. Heard ye the mystic song
Resounding from her caverns as of yore?

Sing to Osiris, for his ark
No more in night profound
Of ocean, fathomless and dark,
Typhon has sunk! Aloud the sistrums ring—
Osiris!—to our god Osiris sing!—
And let the midnight shore to rites of joy resound!

Thee, great restorer of the world, the song
Darkly described, and that mysterious shrine
That bore thee o'er the desolate abyss,
When the earth sank with all its noise!

So taught,
The borderers of the Erithræan launch'd
Their barks, and to the shores of Araby
First their brief voyage stretched, and thence returned
With aromatic gums, or spicy wealth
Of India. Prouder triumphs yet await,
For lo! where Ophir's gold unburied shines
New to the sun; but perilous the way,
O'er Ariana's spectred wilderness,
Where ev'n the patient camel scarce endures
The long, long solitude of rocks and sands,
Parched, faint, and sinking, in his mid-day course.

But see! upon the shore great Ammon stands—
Be the deep opened! At his voice the deep
Is opened; and the shading ships that ride
With statelier masts and ampler hulls the seas,
Have passed the Straits, and left the rocks and GATES
OF DEATH. Where Asia's cape the autumnal surge
Throws blackening back, beneath a hollow cove,
Awhile the mariners their fearful course
Ponder, ere yet they tempt the further deep;
Then plunged into the sullen main, they cast
The youthful victim, to the dismal gods
Devoted, whilst the smoke of sacrifice
Slowly ascends:

Hear, King of Ocean! hear,
Dark phantom! whether in thy secret cave
Thou sittest, where the deeps are fathomless,
Nor hear'st the waters hum, though all above
Is uproar loud; or on the widest waste,
Far from all land, mov'st in the noontide sun,
With dread and lonely shadow; or on high
Dost ride upon the whirling spires, and fume
Of that enormous volume, that ascends

Black to the skies, and with the thunder's roar
Bursts, while the waves far on are still: Oh, hear,
Dread power, and save! lest hidden eddies whirl
The helpless vessels down,—down to the deeps
Of night, where thou, O Father of the Storm,
Dost sleep; or thy vast stature might appear
High o'er the flashing waves, and (as thy beard
Streamed to the cloudy winds) pass o'er their track,
And they are seen no more; or monster-birds
Darkening, with pennons lank, the morn, might bear
The victims to some desert rock, and leave
Their scattered bones to whiten in the winds!

The Ocean-gods, with sacrifice appeased,
Propitious smile; the thunder's roar has ceased,
Smooth and in silence o'er the azure realm
The tall ships glide along; for the South-West
Cheerly and steady blows, and the blue seas
Beneath the shadow sparkle; on they speed,
The long coast varies as they pass from cove
To sheltering cove, the long coast winds away;
Till now emboldened by the unvarying gale,
Still urging to the East, the sailors deem
Some god inviting swells their willing sails,
Or Destiny's fleet dragons through the surge
Cut their mid-way, yoked to the beaked prows
Unseen!

Night after night the heavens' still cope,
That glows with stars, they watch, till morning bears
Airs of sweet fragrance o'er the yellow tide:
Then Malabar her green declivities
Hangs beauteous, beaming to the eye afar
Like scenes of pictured bliss, the shadowy land
Of soft enchantment. Now Salmala's peak
Shines high in air, and Ceylon's dark green woods
Beneath are spread; while, as the strangers wind
Along the curving shores, sounds of delight
Are heard; and birds of richest plumage, red
And yellow, glance along the shades; or fly
With morning twitter, circling o'er the mast,
As singing welcome to the weary crew.
Here rest, till westering gales again invite.
Then o'er the line of level seas glide on,
As the green deities of ocean guide,
Till Ophir's distant hills spring from the main,
And their long labours cease.

Hence Asia slow
Her length unwinds; and Siam and Ceylon
Through wider channels pour their gems and gold
To swell the pomp of Egypt's kings, or deck
With new magnificence the rising dome
Of Palestine's imperial lord.

His wants
To satisfy; "with comelier draperies"
To clothe his shivering form; to bid his arm
Burst, like the Patagonian's, the vain cords
That bound his untried strength; to nurse the flame
Of wider heart-ennobling sympathies;—
For this young Commerce roused the energies
Of man; else rolling back, stagnant and foul,
Like the GREAT ELEMENT on which his ships
Go forth, without the currents, winds, and tides
That swell it, as with awful life, and keep
From rank putrescence the long-moving mass:
And He, the sovereign Maker of the world,
So to excite man's high activities,
Bad various climes their various produce pour.
On Asia's plain mark where the cotton-tree
Hangs elegant its golden gems; the date
Sits purpling the soft lucid haze, that lights
The still, pale, sultry landscape; breathing sweet
Along old Ocean's billowy marge, the eve
Bears spicy fragrance far; the bread-fruit shades
The southern isles; and gems, and richest ore,
Lurk in the caverned mountains of the west.
With ampler shade the northern oak uplifts
His strength, itself a forest, and descends
Proud to the world of waves, to bear afar
The wealth collected, on the swelling tides,
To every land:—Where nature seems to mourn
Her rugged outcast rocks, there Enterprise
Leaps up; he gazes, like a god, around;
He sees on other plains rich harvests wave;
He marks far off the diamond blaze; he burns
To reach the glittering prize; he looks; he speaks;
The pines of Lebanon fall at his voice;
He rears the towering mast: o'er the long main
He wanders, and becomes, himself though poor,
The sovereign of the globe!

So Sidon rose;
And Tyre, yet prouder o'er the subject waves,—
When in his manlier might the Ammonian spread

Beyond Philistia to the Syrian sands,—
Crowned on her rocky citadel, beheld
The treasures of all lands poured at her feet.
Her daring prows the inland main disclosed;
Freedom and Glory, Eloquence, and Arts,
Follow their track, upspringing where they passed;
Till, lo! another Thebes, an ATHENS springs,
From the Ægean shores, and airs are heard,
As of no mortal melody, from isles
That strew the deep around! On to the STRAITS
Where tower the brazen pillars to the clouds,
Her vessels ride. But what a shivering dread
Quelled their bold hopes, when on their watch by night
The mariners first saw the distant flames
Of Ætna, and its red portentous glare
Streaking the midnight waste! 'Tis not thy lamp,
Astarte, hung in the dun vault of night,
To guide the wanderers of the main! Aghast
They eye the fiery cope, and wait the dawn.
Huge pitchy clouds upshoot, and bursting fires
Flash through the horrid volume as it mounts;
Voices are heard, and thunders muttering deep.
Haste, snatch the oars, fly o'er the glimmering surge—
Fly far—already louder thunders roll,
And more terrific flames arise! Oh, spare,
Dread Power! for sure some deity abides
Deep in the central earth, amidst the reek
Of sacrifice and blue sulphureous fume
Involved. Perhaps the living Moloch there
Rules in his horrid empire, amid flames,
Thunders, and blackening volumes, that ascend
And wrap his burning throne!

So was their path,
To those who first the cheerless ocean roamed,
Darkened with dread and peril. Scylla here,
And fell Charybdis, on their whirling gulph
Sit, like the sisters of Despair, and howl,
As the devoted ship, dashed on the crags,
Goes down: and oft the neighbour shores are strewn
With bones of strangers sacrificed, whose bark
Has foundered nigh, where the red watch-tower glares
Through darkness. Hence mysterious dread, and tales
Of Polyphemus and his monstrous rout;
And warbling syrens on the fatal shores
Of soft Parthenope. Yet oft the sound
Of sea-conch through the night from some rude rock
Is heard, to warn the wandering passenger

Of fiends that lurk for blood!

These dangers past,
The sea puts on new beauties: Italy,
Beneath the blue soft sky beaming afar,
Opens her azure bays; Liguria's gulph
Is past; the Bætic rocks, and ramparts high,
That CLOSE THE WORLD, appear. The dashing bark
Bursts through the fearful frith: Ah! all is now
One boundless billowy waste; the huge-heaved wave
Beneath the keel turns more intensely blue;
And vaster rolls the surge, that sweeps the shores
Of Cerne, and the green Hesperides,
And long-renowned Atlantis, whether sunk
Now to the bottom of the "monstróus world;"
Or was it but a shadow of the mind,
Vapoury and baseless, like the distant clouds
That seem the promise of an unknown land
To the pale-eyed and wasted mariner,
Cold on the rocking mast. The pilot plies,
Now tossed upon Bayonna's mountain-surge,
High to the north his way; when, lo! the cliffs
Of Albion, o'er the sea-line rising calm
And white, and Marazion's woody mount
Lifting its dark romantic point between.

So did thy ships to Earth's wide bounds proceed,
O Tyre! and thou wert rich and beautiful
In that thy day of glory. Carthage rose,
Thy daughter, and the rival of thy fame,
Upon the sands of Lybia; princes were
Thy merchants; on thy golden throne thy state
Shone, like the orient sun. Dark Lebanon
Waved all his pines for thee; for thee the oaks
Of Bashan towered in strength: thy galleys cut,
Glittering, the sunny surge; thy mariners,
On ivory benches, furled th' embroidered sails,
That looms of Egypt wove, or to the oars,
That measuring dipped, their choral sea-songs sung;
The multitude of isles did shout for thee,
And cast their emeralds at thy feet, and said—
Queen of the Waters, who is like to thee!

So wert thou glorious on the seas, and said'st,
I am a God, and there is none like me.
But the dread voice prophetic is gone forth:—
Howl, for the whirlwind of the desert comes!
Howl ye again, for Tyre, her multitude

Of sins and dark abominations cry
Against her, saith the LORD; in the mid seas
Her beauty shall be broken; I will bring
Her pride to ashes; she shall be no more,
The distant isles shall tremble at the sound
When thou dost fall; the princes of the sea
Shall from their thrones come down, and cast away
Their gorgeous robes; for thee they shall take up
A bitter lamentation, and shall say—
How art thou fallen, renowned city! THOU,
Who wert enthroned glorious on the seas,
To rise no more!

So visible, O GOD,
Is thy dread hand in all the earth! Where Tyre
In gold and purple glittered o'er the scene,
Now the poor fisher dries his net, nor thinks
How great, how rich, how glorious, once she rose!
Meantime the furthest isle, cold and obscure,
Whose painted natives roamed their woody wilds,
From all the world cut off, that wondering marked
Her stately sails approach, now in her turn
Rises a star of glory in the West—
Albion, the wonder of the illumined world!
See there a Newton wing the highest heavens;
See there a Herschell's daring hand withdraw
The luminous pavilion, and the throne
Of the bright SUN reveal; there hear the voice
Of holy truth amid her cloistered fane,
As the clear anthem swells; see Taste adorn
Her palaces; and Painting's fervid touch,
That bids the canvas breathe; hear angel-strains,
When Handel, or melodious Purcell, pours
His sweetest harmonies; see Poesy
Open her vales romantic, and the scenes
Where Fancy, an enraptured votary, roves
At eve; and hark! 'twas Shakspeare's voice! he sits
Upon a high and charmed rock alone,
And, like the genius of the mountain, gives
The rapt song to the winds; whilst Pity weeps,
Or Terror shudders at the changeful tones,
As when his Ariel soothes the storm! Then pause,
For the wild billows answer—Lycidas
Is dead, young Lycidas, dead ere his prime,
Whelmed in the deep, beyond the Orcades,
Or where the "vision of the guarded Mount,
BELERUS holds."

Nor skies, nor earth, confine
The march of England's glory; on she speeds—
The unknown barriers of the utmost deep
Her prow has burst, where the dread genius slept
For ages undisturbed, save when he walked
Amid the darkness of the storm! Her fleet
Even now along the East rides terrible,
Where early-rising commerce cheered the scene!
Heard ye the thunders of her vengeance roll,
As Nelson, through the battle's dark-red haze
Aloft upon the burning prow directs,
Where the dread hurricane, with sulphureous flash,
Shall burst unquenchable, while from the grave
Osiris ampler seems to rise? Where thou,
O Tyre! didst awe the subject seas of yore,
Acre even now, and ancient Carmel, hears
The cry of conquest. 'Mid the fire and smoke
Of the war-shaken citadel, with eye
Of temper'd flame, yet resolute command,
His brave sword beaming, and his cheering voice
Heard 'mid the onset's cries, his dark-brown hair
Spread on his fearless forehead, and his hand
Pointing to Gallia's baffled chief, behold
The British Hero stand! Why beats my heart
With kindred animation? The warm tear
Of patriot triumph fills mine eye. I strike
A louder strain unconscious, while the harp
Swells to the bold involuntary song.

I.
Fly, SON OF TERROR, fly!
Back o'er the burning desert he is fled!
In heaps the gory dead
And livid in the trenches lie!
His dazzling files no more
Flash on the Syrian sands,
As when from Egypt's ravaged shore,
Aloft their gleamy falchions swinging,
Aloud their victor pæans singing,
Their onward way the Gallic legions took.
Despair, dismay, are on his altered look,
Yet hate indignant lowers;
Whilst high on Acre's granite towers
The shade of English Richard seems to stand;
And frowning far, in dusky rows,
A thousand archers draw their bows!
They join the triumph of the British band,

And the rent watch-tower echoes to the cry,
Heard o'er the rolling surge—They fly, they fly!

II.
Now the hostile fires decline,
Now through the smoke's deep volumes shine;
Now above the bastions gray
The clouds of battle roll away;
Where, with calm, yet glowing mien,
Britain's victorious youth is seen!
He lifts his eye,
His country's ensigns wave through smoke on high,
Whilst the long-mingled shout is heard—They fly, they fly!

III.
Hoary CARMEL, witness thou,
And lift in conscious pride thy brow;
As when upon thy cloudy plain
BAAL'S PROPHETS cried in vain!
They gashed their flesh, and leaped, and cried,
From morn till lingering even-tide.
Then stern ELIJAH on his foes
Strong in the might of Heaven arose!—
On CARMEL'S top he stood,
And while the blackening clouds and rain
Came sounding from the Western main,
Raised his right hand that dropped with impious blood.
ANCIENT KISHON prouder swell,
On whose banks they bowed, they fell,
The mighty ones of yore, when, pale with dread,
Inglorious SISERA fled!
So let them perish, Holy LORD,
Who for OPPRESSION lift the sword;
But let all those who, armed for freedom, fight,
"Be as the sun who goes forth in his might."

NOTES

Alluding to the harps found in the caverns of Thebes.

Migdol was a fortress which guarded the pass of Egypt; Baal-zephon, a sea idol, generally considered the guardian of the coast.

The Cushites inhabited the granite rocks stretching along the Red Sea.

When the Egyptians found the ark, their expression was, "Let us rejoice, we have found the lost Osiris," or Noah.

The deluge or devastating storm.

The desert of Ariana, where the army of Cyrus perished.

Ammon, according to Sir Isaac Newton, was the first artificer who built large ships, and passed the Straits.

The entrance into the Red Sea was called the Gate of Affliction.

Temple of Solomon.

Alluding to the story of Patagonians bursting their cords when taken.

Pillars of Hercules.

Moloch, whose rites of blood are well known, was worshipped along the coast of Syria.

The island described by Plato; by some supposed to be America.

BOOK THE THIRD

My heart has sighed in secret, when I thought
That the dark tide of time might one day close,
England, o'er thee, as long since it has closed
On Egypt and on Tyre: that ages hence,
From the Pacific's billowy loneliness,
Whose tract thy daring search revealed, some isle
Might rise in green-haired beauty eminent,
And like a goddess, glittering from the deep,
Hereafter sway the sceptre of domain
From pole to pole; and such as now thou art,
Perhaps NEW-HOLLAND be. For who shall say
What the OMNIPOTENT ETERNAL ONE,
That made the world, hath purposed! Thoughts like these,
Though visionary, rise; and sometimes move
A moment's sadness, when I think of thee,
My country, of thy greatness, and thy name,
Among the nations; and thy character,—
Though some few spots be on thy flowing robe,—
Of loveliest beauty: I have never passed
Through thy green hamlets on a summer's morn,
Nor heard thy sweet bells ring, nor seen the youths
And smiling maidens of thy villages,

Gay in their Sunday tire, but I have said,
With passing tenderness—Live, happy land,
Where the poor peasant feels his shed, though small,
An independence and a pride, that fill
His honest heart with joy—joy such as they
Who crowd the mart of men may never feel!
Such, England, is thy boast. When I have heard
The roar of ocean bursting 'round thy rocks,
Or seen a thousand thronging masts aspire,
Far as the eye could reach, from every port
Of every nation, streaming with their flags
O'er the still mirror of the conscious Thames,—
Yes, I have felt a proud emotion swell
That I was British-born; that I had lived
A witness of thy glory, my most loved
And honoured country; and a silent prayer
Would rise to Heaven, that Fame and Peace, and Love
And Liberty, might walk thy vales, and sing
Their holy hymns, while thy brave arm repelled
Hostility, even as thy guardian cliffs
Repel the dash of that dread element
Which calls me, lingering on the banks of Thames,
On to my destined voyage, by the shores
Of Asia, and the wreck of cities old,
Ere yet we burst into the wilder deep
With Gama; or the huge Atlantic waste
With bold Columbus stem; or view the bounds
Of field-ice, stretching to the southern pole,
With thee, benevolent, lamented Cook!
Tyre be no more! said the ALMIGHTY voice:
But thou too, Monarch of the world, whose arm
Rent the proud bulwarks of the golden queen
Of cities, throned upon her subject seas,
ART THOU TOO FALL'N?

The whole earth is at rest:
"They break forth into singing:" Lebanon
Waves all his hoary pines, and seems to say,
No feller now comes here; HELL from beneath
Is moved to meet thy coming; it stirs up
The DEAD for thee; the CHIEF ONES of the earth,
Tyre and the nations, they all speak and say—
Art thou become like us! Thy pomp brought down
E'en to the dust! The noise of viols ceased,
The worm spread under thee, the crawling worm
To cover thee! How art thou fall'n from heaven,
Son of the morning! In thy heart thou saidst,
I will ascend to Heaven; I will exalt

My throne above the stars of God! Die—die,
Blasphemer! As a carcase under foot,
Defiled and trodden, so be thou cast out!
And SHE, the great, the guilty Babel—SHE
Who smote the wasted cities, and the world
Made as a wilderness—SHE, in her turn,
Sinks to the gulf oblivious at the voice
Of HIM who sits in judgment on her crimes!
Who, o'er her palaces and buried towers,
Shall bid the owl hoot, and the bittern scream;
And on her pensile groves and pleasant shades
Pour the deep waters of forgetfulness.

On that same night, when with a cry she fell,
(Like her own mighty idol dashed to earth,)
There was a strange eclipse, and long laments
Were heard, and muttering thunders o'er the towers
Of the high palace where his wassail loud
Belshazzar kept, mocking the GOD OF HEAVEN,
And flushed with impious mirth; for BEL had left
With sullen shriek his golden shrine, and sat,
With many a gloomy apparition girt,
NISROCH and NEBO chief, in the dim sphere
Of mooned ASTORETH, whose orb now rolled
In darkness:—They their earthly empire mourned;
Meantime the host of Cyrus through the night
Silent advanced more nigh; and at that hour,
In the torch-blazing hall of revelry,
The fingers of a shadowy hand distinct
Came forth, and unknown figures marked the wall,
Searing the eye-balls of the starting king:
Tyre is avenged; Babel is fall'n, is fall'n!
Bel and her gods are shattered!

PRINCE, to thee
Called by the voice of God to execute
His will on earth, and raised to Persia's throne,
CYRUS, all hearts pay homage. Touched with tints
Most clear by the historian's magic art,
Thy features wear a gentleness and grace
Unlike the stern cold aspect and the frown
Of the dark chiefs of yore, the gloomy clan
Of heroes, from humanity and love
Removed: To thee a brighter character
Belongs—high dignity, unbending truth—
Yet Nature; not that lordly apathy
Which confidence and human sympathy
Represses, but a soul that bids all hearts

Smiling approach. We almost burn in thought
To kiss the hand that loosed Panthea's chains,
And bless him with a parent's, husband's tear,
Who stood a guardian angel in distress
To the unfriended, and the beautiful,
Consigned a helpless slave. Thy portrait, touched
With tints of softest light, thus wins all hearts
To love thee; but severer policy,
Cyrus, pronounces otherwise: she hears
No stir of commerce on the sullen marge
Of waters that along thy empire's verge
Beat cheerless; no proud moles arise; no ships,
Freighted with Indian wealth, glide o'er the main
From cape to cape. But on the desert sands
Hurtles thy numerous host, seizing, in thought
Rapacious, the rich fields of Hindostan,
As the poor savage fells the blooming tree
To gain its tempting fruit; but woe the while!
For in the wilderness the noise is lost
Of all thy archers;—they have ceased;—the wind
Blows o'er them, and the voice of judgment cries:
So perish they who grasp with avarice
Another's blessed portion, and disdain
That interchange of mutual good, that crowns
The slow, sure toil of commerce.

It was thine,
Immortal son of Macedon! to hang
In the high fane of maritime renown
The fairest trophies of thy fame, and shine,
THEN only like a god, when thy great mind
Swayed in its master council the deep tide
Of things, predestining th' eventful roll
Of commerce, and uniting either world,
Europe and Asia, in thy vast design.

Twas when the victor, in his proud career,
O'er ravaged Hindostan, had now advanced
Beyond Hydaspes; on the flowery banks
Of Hyphasis, with banners thronged, his camp
Was spread. On high he bade the altars rise,
The awful records to succeeding years
Of his long march of glory, and to point
The spot where, like the thunder rolled away,
His army paused. Now shady eve came down;
The trumpet sounded to the setting sun,
That looked from his illumed pavilion, calm
Upon the scene of arms, as if, all still,

And lovely as his parting light, the world
Beneath him spread; nor clangours, nor deep groans,
Were heard, nor victory's shouts, nor sighs, nor shrieks,
Were ever wafted from a bleeding land,
After the havoc of a conqueror's sword.
So calm the sun declined; when from the woods,
That shone to his last beam, a Brahmin old
Came forth. His streaming beard shone in the ray,
That slanted o'er his feeble frame; his front
Was furrowed. To the sun's last light he cast
A look of sorrow, then in silence bowed
Before the conqueror of the world. At once
All, as in death, was still. The victor chief
Trembled, he knew not why; the trumpet ceased
Its clangor, and the crimson streamer waved
No more in folds insulting to the Lord
Of the reposing world. The pallid front
Of the meek man seemed for a moment calm,
Yet dark and thronging thoughts appeared to swell
His beating heart. He paused—and then abrupt:

Victor, avaunt! he cried,
Hence! and the banners of thy pride
Bear to the deep! Behold on high
Yon range of mountains mingled with the sky!

It is the place
Where the great Father of the human race
Rested, when all the world and all its sounds
Ceased; and the ocean that surrounds
The earth, leaped from its dark abode
Beneath the mountains, and enormous flowed,
The green earth deluging! List, soldier, list!
And dread His might no mortal may resist.

Great Bramah rested, hushed in sleep,
When Hayagraiva came,
With mooned horns and eyes of flame,
And bore the holy Vedas to the deep.
Far from the sun's rejoicing ray,
Beneath the huge abyss, the buried treasures lay.
Then foamed the billowy desert wide,
And all that breathed—they died,
Sunk in the rolling waters: such the crime
And violence of earth. But he above,
Great Vishnu, moved with pitying love,
Preserved the pious king, whose ark sublime
Floated, in safety borne:

For his stupendous horn,
Blazing like gold, and many a rood
Extended o'er the dismal flood,
The precious freight sustained, till on the crest
Of Himakeel, yon mountain high,
That darkly mingles with the sky,
Where many a griffin roams, the hallowed ark found rest.
And Heaven decrees that here
Shall cease thy slaughtering spear:
Enough we bleed, enough we weep,
Hence, victor, to the deep!
Ev'n now along the tide
I see thy ships triumphant ride:
I see the world of trade emerge
From ocean's solitude! What fury fires
My breast! The flood, the flood retires,
And owns its future sovereign! Urge
Thy destined way; what countless pennants stream!
(Or is it but the shadow of a dream?)
Ev'n now old Indus hails
Thy daring prows in long array,
That o'er the lone seas gliding,
Around the sea-gods riding,
Speed to Euphrates' shores their destined way.
Fill high the bowl of mirth!
From west to east the earth
Proclaims thee Lord; shall the blue main
Confine thy reign?
But tremble, tyrant; hark in many a ring,
With language dread
Above thy head,
The dark Assoors thy death-song sing.
What mortal blow
Hath laid the king of nations low?
No hand: his own despair.—
But shout, for the canvas shall swell to the air,
Thy ships explore
Unknown Persia's winding shore,
While the great dragon rolls his arms in vain.
And see, uprising from the level main,
A new and glorious city springs;—
Hither speed thy woven wings,
That glance along the azure tide;
Asia and Europe own thy might;—
The willing seas of either world unite:
Thy name shall consecrate the sands,
And glittering to the sky the mart of nations stands.
He spoke, and rushed into the thickest wood.

With flashing eyes the impatient monarch cried—
Yes, by the Lybian Ammon and the gods
Of Greece, thou bid'st me on, the self-same track
My spirit pointed; and, let death betide,
My name shall live in glory!

At his word
The pines descend; the thronging masts aspire;
The novel sails swell beauteous o'er the curves
Of INDUS; to the Moderators' song
The oars keep time, while bold Nearchus guides
Aloft the gallies. On the foremost prow
The monarch from his golden goblet pours
A full libation to the gods, and calls
By name the mighty rivers, through whose course
He seeks the sea. To Lybian Ammon loud
The songs ascend; the trumpets bray; aloft
The streamers fly, whilst on the evening wave
Majestic to the main the fleet descends.

NOTES

Nebuchadnezzar, the destroyer of Tyre.

Hayagraiva, the evil spirit of the ocean.

The sacred writings of the Hindus.

Caucasus.

Alluding to the astonishment of Alexander's soldiers, when they first witnessed the effects of the tide.

Assoors, the evil genii of India.

Moderators were people stationed on the poop, to excite with songs the maritime ardour, while the oars kept time.

BOOK THE FOURTH

Stand on the gleaming Pharos, and aloud
Shout, Commerce, to the kingdoms of the earth;
Shout, for thy golden portals are set wide,
And all thy streamers o'er the surge, aloft,
In pomp triumphant wave. The weary way
That pale Nearchus passed, from creek to creek

Advancing slow, no longer bounds the track
Of the adventurous mariner, who steers
Steady, with eye intent upon the stars,
To Elam's echoing port. Meantime, more high
Aspiring, o'er the Western main her towers
Th' imperial city lifts, the central mart
Of nations, and beneath the calm clear sky,
At distance from the palmy marge, displays
Her clustering columns, whitening to the morn.

Damascus' fleece, Golconda's gems, are there.
Murmurs the haven with one ceaseless hum;
The hurrying camel's bell, the driver's song,
Along the sands resound. Tyre, art thou fall'n?
A prouder city crowns the inland sea,
Raised by his hand who smote thee; as if thus
His mighty mind were swayed to recompense
The evil of his march through cities stormed,
And regions wet with blood! and still had flowed
The tide of commerce through the destined track,
Traced by his mind sagacious, who surveyed
The world he conquered with a sage's eye,
As with a soldier's spirit; but a scene
More awful opens: ancient world, adieu!
Adieu, cloud-piercing pillars, erst its bounds;
And thou, whose aged head once seemed to prop
The heavens, huge Atlas, sinking fast, adieu!
What though the seas with wilder fury rave,
Through their deserted realm; though the dread Cape,
Sole-frowning o'er the war of waves below,
That bar the seaman's search, horrid in air
Appear with giant amplitude; his head
Shrouded in clouds, the tempest at his feet,
And standing thus terrific, seem to say,
Incensed—Approach who dare! What though the fears
Of superstition people the vexed space
With spirits unblessed, that lamentations make
To the sad surge beyond—yet Enterprise,
Not now a darkling Cyclop on the sands
Striding, but led by Science, and advanced
To a more awful height, on the wide scene
Looks down commanding.

Does a shuddering thought
Of danger start, as the tumultuous sea
Tosses below! Calm Science, with a smile,
Displays the wondrous index, that still points,
With nice vibration tremulous, to the Pole.

And such, she whispers, is the just man's hope
In this tempestuous scene of human things;
Even as the constant needle to the North
Still points; so Piety and meek-eyed Faith
Direct, though trembling oft, their constant gaze
Heavenward, as to their lasting home, nor fear
The night, fast closing on their earthly way.

And guided by this index, thou shall pass
The world of seas secure. Far from all land,
Where not a sea-bird wanders; where nor star,
Nor moon appears, nor the bright noonday sun,
Safe in the wildering storm, as when the breeze
Of summer gently blows; through day, through night,
Where sink the well-known stars, and others rise
Slow from the South, the victor bark shall ride.

Henry! thy ardent mind first pierced the gloom
Of dark disastrous ignorance, that sat
Upon the Southern wave, like the deep cloud
That lowered upon the woody skirts, and veiled
From mortal search, with umbrage ominous,
Madeira's unknown isle. But look! the morn
Is kindled on the shadowy offing; streaks
Of clear cold light on Sagres' battlements
Are cast, where Henry watches, listening still
To the unwearied surge; and turning still
His anxious eyes to the horizon's bounds.
A sail appears; it swells, it shines: more high
Seen through the dusk it looms; and now the hull
Is black upon the surge, whilst she rolls on
Aloft—the weather-beaten ship—and now
Streams by the watch-tower!

Zarco, from the deep
What tidings?

The loud storm of night prevailed,
And swept our vessel from Bojador's rocks
Far out to sea; a sylvan isle received
Our sails; so willed the ALMIGHTY—He who speaks,
And all the waves are still!

Hail, HENRY cried,
The omen: we have burst the sole barrier,
(Prosper our wishes, Father of the world!)
We speed to Asia.

Soon upon the deep
The brave ship speeds again. Bojador's rocks
Arise at distance, frowning o'er the surf,
That boils for many a league without. Its course
The ship holds on; till lo! the beauteous isle,
That shielded late the sufferers from the storm,
Springs o'er the wave again. Here they refresh
Their wasted strength, and lift their vows to Heaven,
But Heaven denies their further search; for ah!
What fearful apparition, palled in clouds,
For ever sits upon the Western wave,
Like night, and in its strange portentous gloom
Wrapping the lonely waters, seems the bounds
Of Nature? Still it sits, day after day,
The same mysterious vision. Holy saints!
Is it the dread abyss where all things cease?
Or haply hid from mortal search, thine isle,
Cipango, and that unapproached seat
Of peace, where rest the Christians whom the hate
Of Moorish pride pursued? Whate'er it be,
Zarco, thy holy courage bids thee on
To burst the gloom, though dragons guard the shore,
Or beings more than mortal pace the sands.

The favouring gales invite; the bowsprit bears
Right onward to the fearful shade; more black
The cloudy spectre towers; already fear
Shrinks at the view aghast and breathless. Hark!
'Twas more than the deep murmur of the surge
That struck the ear; whilst through the lurid gloom
Gigantic phantoms seem to lift in air
Their misty arms; yet, yet—bear boldly on—
The mist dissolves;—seen through the parting haze,
Romantic rocks, like the depictured clouds,
Shine out; beneath a blooming wilderness
Of varied wood is spread, that scents the air;
Where fruits of "golden rind," thick interspersed
And pendent, through the mantling umbrage gleam
Inviting. Cypress here, and stateliest pine,
Spire o'er the nether shades, as emulous
Of sole distinction where all nature smiles.
Some trees, in sunny glades alone their head
And graceful stem uplifting, mark below
The turf with shadow; whilst in rich festoons
The flowery lianes braid their boughs; meantime
Choirs of innumerous birds of liveliest song
And brightest plumage, flitting through the shades,
With nimble glance are seen; they, unalarmed,

Now near in airy circles sing, then speed
Their random flight back to their sheltering bowers,
Whose silence, broken only by their song,
From the foundation of this busy world,
Perhaps had never echoed to the voice,
Or heard the steps, of Man. What rapture fired
The strangers' bosoms, as from glade to glade
They passed, admiring all, and gazing still
With new delight! 'Tis solitude around;
Deep solitude, that on the gloom of woods
Primæval fearful hangs: a green recess
Now opens in the wilderness; gay flowers
Of unknown name purple the yielding sward;
The ring-dove murmurs o'er their head, like one
Attesting tenderest joy; but mark the trees,
Where, slanting through the gloom, the sunshine rests!
Beneath, a moss-grown monument appears,
O'er which the green banana gently waves
Its long leaf; and an aged cypress near
Leans, as if listening to the streamlet's sound,
That gushes from the adverse bank; but pause—
Approach with reverence! Maker of the world,
There is a Christian's cross! and on the stone
A name, yet legible amid its moss,—
Anna!

In that remote, sequestered spot,
Shut as it seemed from all the world, and lost
In boundless seas, to trace a name, to mark
The emblems of their holy faith, from all
Drew tears; while every voice faintly pronounced,
Anna! But thou, loved harp! whose strings have rung
To louder tones, oh! let my hand, awhile,
The wires more softly touch, whilst I rehearse
Her name and fate, who in this desert deep,
Far from the world, from friends, and kindred, found
Her long and last abode; there where no eye
Might shed a tear on her remains; no heart
Sigh in remembrance of her fate:—

She left
The Severn's side, and fled with him she loved
O'er the wide main; for he had told her tales
Of happiness in distant lands, where care
Comes not; and pointing to the golden clouds
That shone above the waves, when evening came,
Whispered—Oh, are there not sweet scenes of peace,
Far from the murmurs of this cloudy mart,—

Where gold alone bears sway,—scenes of delight,
Where love may lay his head upon the lap
Of innocence, and smile at all the toil
Of the low-thoughted throng, that place in wealth
Their only bliss! Yes, there are scenes like these.
Leave the vain chidings of the world behind,
Country, and hollow friends, and fly with me
Where love and peace in distant vales invite.
What wouldst thou here! Oh, shall thy beauteous look
Of maiden innocence, thy smile of youth, thine eyes
Of tenderness and soft subdued desire,
Thy form, thy limbs—oh, madness!—be the prey
Of a decrepit spoiler, and for gold?—
Perish his treasure with him. Haste with me;
We shall find out some sylvan nook, and then,
If thou shouldst sometimes think upon these hills,
When they are distant far, and drop a tear,
Yes—I will kiss it from thy cheek, and clasp
Thy angel beauties closer to my breast;
And whilst the winds blow o'er us, and the sun
Sinks beautifully down, and thy soft cheek
Reclines on mine, I will infold thee thus,
And proudly cry, My friend—my love—my wife!
So tempted he, and soon her heart approved,
Nay wooed, the blissful dream; and oft at eve,
When the moon shone upon the wandering stream,
She paced the castle's battlements, that threw
Beneath their solemn shadow, and, resigned
To fancy and to tears, thought it most sweet
To wander o'er the world with him she loved.
Nor was his birth ignoble, for he shone
'Mid England's gallant youth in Edward's reign:
With countenance erect, and honest eye
Commanding (yet suffused in tenderness
At times), and smiles that like the lightning played
On his brown cheek,—so gently stern he stood,
Accomplished, generous, gentle, brave, sincere,—
Robert a Machin. But the sullen pride
Of haughty D'Arfet scorned all other claim
To his high heritage, save what the pomp
Of amplest wealth and loftier lineage gave.
Reckless of human tenderness, that seeks
One loved, one honoured object, wealth alone
He worshipped; and for this he could consign
His only child, his aged hope, to loathed
Embraces, and a life of tears! Nor here
His hard ambition ended; for he sought,
By secret whispers of conspiracies,

His sovereign to abuse, bidding him lift
His arm avenging, and upon a youth
Of promise close the dark forgotten gates
Of living sepulture, and in the gloom
Inhume the slowly-wasting victim.

So
He purposed, but in vain; the ardent youth
Rescued her—her whom more than life he loved,
Ev'n when the horrid day of sacrifice
Drew nigh. He pointed to the distant bark,
And while he kissed a stealing tear that fell
On her pale cheek, as trusting she reclined
Her head upon his breast, with ardour cried—
Be mine, be only mine! the hour invites;
Be mine, be only mine! So won, she cast
A look of last affection on the towers
Where she had passed her infant days, that now
Shone to the setting sun. I follow thee,
Her faint voice said; and lo! where in the air
A sail hangs tremulous, and soon her feet
Ascend the vessel's side: The vessel glides
Down the smooth current, as the twilight fades,
Till soon the woods of Severn, and the spot
Where D'Arfet's solitary turrets rose,
Is lost; a tear starts to her eye, she thinks
Of him whose gray head to the earth shall bend,
When he speaks nothing—but be all, like death,
Forgotten. Gently blows the placid breeze,
And oh! that now some fairy pinnace light
Might flit across the wave (by no seen power
Directed, save when Love upon the prow
Gathered or spread with tender hand the sail),
That now some fairy pinnace, o'er the surge
Silent, as in a summer's dream, might waft
The passengers upon the conscious flood
To regions bright of undisturbed joy!

But hark!
The wind is in the shrouds;—the cordage sings
With fitful violence;—the blast now swells,
Now sinks. Dread gloom invests the further wave,
Whose foaming toss alone is seen, beneath
The veering bowsprit.

Oh, retire to rest,
Maiden, whose tender heart would beat, whose cheek
Turn pale to see another thus exposed!

Hark! the deep thunder louder peals—Oh, save!—
The high mast crashes; but the faithful arm
Of love is o'er thee, and thy anxious eye,
Soon as the gray of morning peeps, shall view
Green Erin's hills aspiring!

The sad morn
Comes forth; but terror on the sunless wave
Still, like a sea-fiend, sits, and darkly smiles
Beneath the flash that through the struggling clouds
Bursts frequent, half revealing his scathed front,
Above the rocking of the waste that rolls
Boundless around.

No word through the long day
She spoke;—another slowly came;—no word
The beauteous drooping mourner spoke. The sun
Twelve times had sunk beneath the sullen surge,
And cheerless rose again:—Ah, where are now
Thy havens, France! But yet—resign not yet—
Ye lost seafarers—oh, resign not yet
All hope—the storm is passed; the drenched sail
Shines in the passing beam! Look up, and say—
Heaven, thou hast heard our prayers!

And lo! scarce seen,
A distant dusky spot appears;—they reach
An unknown shore, and green and flowery vales,
And azure hills, and silver-gushing streams,
Shine forth; a Paradise, which Heaven alone,
Who saw the silent anguish of despair,
Could raise in the waste wilderness of waves.
They gain the haven; through untrodden scenes,
Perhaps untrodden by the foot of man
Since first the earth arose, they wind. The voice
Of Nature hails them here with music, sweet,
As waving woods retired, or falling streams,
Can make; most soothing to the weary heart,
Doubly to those who, struggling with their fate,
And wearied long with watchings and with grief,
Seek but a place of safety. All things here
Whisper repose and peace; the very birds
That 'mid the golden fruitage glance their plumes,
The songsters of the lonely valley, sing—
Welcome from scenes of sorrow, live with us.

The wild wood opens, and a shady glen
Appears, embowered with mantling laurels high,

That sloping shade the flowery valley's side;
A lucid stream, with gentle murmur, strays
Beneath the umbrageous multitude of leaves,
Till gaining, with soft lapse, the nether plain,
It glances light along its yellow bed;—
The shaggy inmates of the forest lick
The feet of their new guests, and gazing stand.
A beauteous tree upshoots amid the glade
Its trembling top; and there upon the bank
They rest them, while each heart o'erflows with joy.

Now evening, breathing richer odours sweet,
Came down: a softer sound the circling seas,
The ancient woods resounded, while the dove,
Her murmurs interposing, tenderness
Awaked, yet more endearing, in the hearts
Of those who, severed wide from human kind,
Woman and man, by vows sincere betrothed,
Heard but the voice of Nature. The still moon
Arose—they saw it not—cheek was to cheek
Inclined, and unawares a stealing tear
Witnessed how blissful was that hour, that seemed
Not of the hours that time could count. A kiss
Stole on the listening silence; ne'er till now
Here heard; they trembled, ev'n as if the Power
That made the world, that planted the first pair
In Paradise, amid the garden walked:—
This since the fairest garden that the world
Has witnessed, by the fabling sons of Greece
Hesperian named, who feigned the watchful guard
Of the scaled Dragon, and the Golden Fruit.
Such was this sylvan Paradise; and here
The loveliest pair, from a hard world remote,
Upon each other's neck reclined; their breath
Alone was heard, when the dove ceased on high
Her plaint; and tenderly their faithful arms
Infolded each the other.

Thou, dim cloud,
That from the search of men these beauteous vales
Hast closed, oh, doubly veil them! But alas,
How short the dream of human transport! Here,
In vain they built the leafy bower of love,
Or culled the sweetest flowers and fairest fruit.
The hours unheeded stole! but ah, not long—
Again the hollow tempest of the night
Sounds through the leaves; the inmost woods resound;
Slow comes the dawn, but neither ship nor sail

Along the rocking of the windy waste
Is seen: the dash of the dark-heaving wave
Alone is heard. Start from your bed of bliss,
Poor victims! never more shall ye behold
Your native vales again; and thou, sweet child!
Who, listening to the voice of love, hast left
Thy friends, thy country,—oh, may the wan hue
Of pining memory, the sunk cheek, the eye
Where tenderness yet dwells, atone (if love
Atonement need, by cruelty and wrong
Beset), atone ev'n now thy rash resolves!
Ah, fruitless hope! Day after day, thy bloom
Fades, and the tender lustre of thy eye
Is dimmed: thy form, amid creation, seems
The only drooping thing.

Thy look was soft,
And yet most animated, and thy step
Light as the roe's upon the mountains. Now,
Thou sittest hopeless, pale, beneath the tree
That fanned its joyous leaves above thy head,
Where love had decked the blooming bower, and strewn
The sweets of summer: DEATH is on thy cheek,
And thy chill hand the pressure scarce returns
Of him, who, agonised and hopeless, hangs
With tears and trembling o'er thee. Spare the sight,—
She faints—she dies!—

He laid her in the earth,
Himself scarce living, and upon her tomb
Beneath the beauteous tree where they reclined,
Placed the last tribute of his earthly love.

INSCRIPTION FOR THE GRAVE OF ANNA D'ARFET.

O'er my poor ANNA'S lowly grave
No dirge shall sound, no knell shall ring;
But angels, as the high pines wave,
Their half-heard "Miserere" sing.

No flowers of transient bloom at eve
The maidens on the turf shall strew;
Nor sigh, as the sad spot they leave,
Sweets to the sweet! a long adieu!

But in this wilderness profound,
O'er her the dove shall build her nest;
And ocean swell with softer sound

A requiem to her dreams of rest!

Ah! when shall I as quiet be,
When not a friend, or human eye,
Shall mark beneath the mossy tree
The spot where we forgotten lie!

To kiss her name on the cold stone,
Is all that now on earth I crave;
For in this world I am alone—
Oh, lay me with her in the grave!

ROBERT A MACHIN.

Miserere nobis, Domine.

He placed the rude inscription on her stone,
Which he with faltering hands had graved, and soon
Himself beside it sunk—yet ere he died,
Faintly he spoke: If ever ye shall hear,
Companions of my few and evil days,
Again the convent's vesper bells, oh! think
Of me; and if in after-times the search
Of men should reach this far removed spot,
Let sad remembrance raise an humble shrine,
And virgin choirs chaunt duly o'er our grave:
Peace, peace! His arm upon the mournful stone
He dropped; his eyes, ere yet in death they closed,
Turned to the name, till he could see no more
ANNA. His pale survivors, earth to earth,
Weeping consigned his poor remains, and placed
Beneath the sod where all he loved was laid.
Then shaping a rude vessel from the woods,
They sought their country o'er the waves, and left
Those scenes once more to deepest solitude.
The beauteous ponciana hung its head
O'er the gray stone; but never human eye
Had mark'd the spot, or gazed upon the grave
Of the unfortunate, but for the voice
Of ENTERPRISE, that spoke, from Sagre's towers,
Through ocean's perils, storms, and unknown wastes—
Speed we to Asia!

Here, Discovery, pause!—
Then from the tomb of him who first was cast
Upon this Heaven-appointed isle, thy gaze
Uplift, and far beyond the Cape of Storms
Pursue De Gama's tract. Mark the rich shores

Of Madagascar, till the purple East
Shines in luxuriant beauty wide disclosed.
But cease thy song, presumptuous Muse!—a bard,
In tones whose patriot sound shall never die,
Has struck his deep shell, and the glorious theme
Recorded.

Say, what lofty meed awaits
The triumph of his victor conch, that swells
Its music on the yellow Tagus' side,
As when Arion, with his glittering harp
And golden hair, scarce sullied from the main,
Bids all the high rocks listen to his voice
Again! Alas, I see an aged form,
An old man worn by penury, his hair
Blown white upon his haggard cheek, his hand
Emaciated, yet the strings with thrilling touch
Soliciting; but the vain crowds pass by:
His very countrymen, whose fame his song
Has raised to heaven, in stately apathy
Wrapped up, and nursed in pride's fastidious lap,
Regard not. As he plays, a sable man
Looks up, but fears to speak, and when the song
Has ceased, kisses his master's feeble hand.
Is that cold wasted hand, that haggard look,
Thine, Camoens? Oh, shame upon the world!
And is there none, none to sustain thee found,
But he, himself unfriended, who so far
Has followed, severed from his native isles,
To scenes of gorgeous cities, o'er the sea,
Thee and thy broken fortunes!

GOD of worlds!
Oh, whilst I hail the triumph and high boast
Of social life, let me not wrong the sense
Of kindness, planted in the human heart
By man's great Maker, therefore I record
Antonio's faithful, gentle, generous love
To his heartbroken master, that might teach,
High as it bears itself, a polished world
More charity.

DISCOVERY, turn thine eyes!
COLUMBUS' toiling ship is on the deep,
Stemming the mid Atlantic.

Waste and wild
The view! On the same sunshine o'er the waves

The murmuring mariners, with languid eye,
Ev'n till the heart is sick, gaze day by day!
At midnight in the wind sad voices sound!
When the slow morning o'er the offing dawns,
Heartless they view the same drear weltering waste
Of seas: and when the sun again goes down
Silent, hope dies within them, and they think
Of parting friendship's last despairing look!
See too, dread prodigy, the needle veers
Her trembling point—will Heaven forsake them too!
But lift thy sunk eye, and thy bloodless look,
Despondence! Milder airs at morning breathe:—
Below the slowly-parting prow the sea
Is dark with weeds; and birds of land are seen
To wing the desert tract, as hasting on
To the green valleys of their distant home.
Yet morn succeeds to morn—and nought around
Is seen, but dark weeds floating many a league,
The sun's sole orb, and the pale hollowness
Of heaven's high arch streaked with the early clouds.
Watchman, what from the giddy mast?

A shade
Appears on the horizon's hazy line.
Land! land! aloud is echoed; but the spot
Fades as the shouting crew delighted gaze—
It fades, and there is nothing—nothing now
But the blue sky, the clouds, and surging seas!
As one who, in the desert, faint with thirst,
Upon the trackless and forsaken sands
Sinks dying; him the burning haze deceives,
As mocking his last torments, while it seems,
To his distempered vision, like th' expanse
Of lucid waters cool: so falsely smiles
Th' illusive land upon the water's edge,
To the long-straining eye showing what seems
Its headlands and its distant trending shores;—
But all is false, and like the pensive dream
Of poor imagination, 'mid the waves
Of troubled life, decked with unreal hues,
And ending soon in emptiness and tears.
'Tis midnight, and the thoughtful chief, retired
From the vexed crowd, in his still cabin hears
The surge that rolls below; he lifts his eyes,
And casts a silent anxious look without.
It is a light—great God—it is a light!
It moves upon the shore!—Land—there is land!
He spoke in secret, and a tear of joy

Stole down his cheek, when on his knees he fell.
Thou, who hast been his guardian in wastes
Of the hoar deep, accept his tears, his prayers;
While thus he fondly hopes the purer light
Of thy great truths on the benighted world
Shall beam!

The lingering night is past;—the sun
Shines out, while now the red-cross streamers wave
High up the gently-surging bay. From all
Shouts, songs, and rapturous thanksgiving loud,
Burst forth: Another world, entranced they cry,
Another living world!—Awe-struck and mute
The gazing natives stand, and drop their spears,
In homage to the gods!

So from the deep
They hail emerging; sight more awful far
Than ever yet the wondering voyager
Greeted;—the prospect of a new-found world,
Now from the night of dark uncertainty
At once revealed in living light!

How beats
The heart! What thronging thoughts awake! Whence sprung
The roaming nations? From that ancient race
That peopled Asia—Noah's sons? How, then,
Passed they the long and lone expanse between
Of stormy ocean, from the elder earth
Cut off, and lost, for unknown ages, lost
In the vast deep? But whilst the awful view
Stands in thy sight revealed, Spirit, awake
To prouder energies! Even now, in thought,
I see thee opening bold Magellan's tract!
The straits are passed! Thou, as the seas expand,
Pausest a moment, when beneath thine eye
Blue, vast, and rocking, through its boundless rule,
The long Pacific stretches. Nor here cease
Thy search, but with De Quiros to the South
Still urge thy way, if yet some continent
Stretch to its dusky pole, with nations spread,
Forests, and hills, and streams.

So be thy search
With ampler views rewarded, till, at length,
Lo, the round world is compassed! Then return
Back to the bosom of the tranquil Thames,
And hail Britannia's victor ship, that now

From many a storm restored, winds its slow way
Silently up the current, and so finds,
Like to a time-worn pilgrim of the world,
Rest, in that haven where all tempests cease.

NOTES

The Pharos was not erected by Alexander, but Alexandria is here supposed to be finished.

Cape Bojador.

John Gongalez Zarco was employed by Prince Henry to conduct the enterprise of discovery along the Western coast of Africa.

Porto Santo.

I have called the three islands of Madeiras the Hesperides, who, in ancient mythology, are the three daughters of Atlas; as I consider the orange-trees and mysterious shade, with the rocks discerned through it on a nearer approach, to be the best solution of the fable of the golden fruit, the dragon, and the three daughters of Atlas.

Magellan's ship first circumnavigated the globe, passing through the straits, called by his name, into the South Sea, and proceeding West to the East Indies. He himself, like our revered Cooke, perished in the enterprise.

De Quiros first discovered the New Hebrides, in the South Sea; afterwards explored by Cooke, who bears testimony to the accuracy of De Quiros. These islands were supposed part of a great continent stretching to the South pole, called Terra Australis incognita.

Drake's ship, in which he sailed round the world; she was laid up at Deptford—hence Ben Johnson, in Every Man in his Humour, "O Coz, it cannot be altered, go not about it; Drake's old ship at Deptford may sooner circle the world again."

BOOK THE FIFTH

Such are thy views, DISCOVERY! The great world
Rolls to thine eye revealed; to thee the Deep
Submits its awful empire; Industry
Awakes, and Commerce to the echoing marts
From east to west unwearied pours her wealth.
Man walks sublimer; and Humanity,
Matured by social intercourse, more high,
More animated, lifts her sovereign mien,
And waves her golden sceptre. Yet the heart
Asks trembling, is no evil found! Oh, turn,

Meek Charity, and drop a human tear
For the sad fate of Afric's injured sons,
And hide, for ever hide, the sight of chains,
Anguish, and bondage! Yes, the heart of man
Is sick, and Charity turns pale, to think
How soon, for pure religion's holy beam,
Dark crimes, that sullied the sweet day, pursued,
Like vultures, the Discoverer's ocean tract,
Screaming for blood, to fields of rich Peru,
Or ravaged Mexico, while Gold more Gold!
The caverned mountains echoed, Gold more Gold!

Then see the fell-eyed, prowling buccaneer,
Grim as a libbard! He his jealous look
Turns to the dagger at his belt, his hand
By instinct grasps a bloody scymitar,
And ghastly is his smile, as o'er the woods
He sees the smoke of burning villages
Ascend, and thinks ev'n now he counts his spoil.

See thousands destined to the lurid mine,
Never to see the sun again; all names
Of husband, sire, all tender charities
Of love, deep buried with them in that grave,
Where life is as a thing long passed; and hope
No more its sickly ray, to cheer the gloom,
Extends.

Thou, too, dread Ocean, toss thine arms,
Exulting, for the treasures and the gems
That thy dark oozy realm emblaze; and call
The pale procession of the dead, from caves
Where late their bodies weltered, to attend
Thy kingly sceptre, and proclaim thy might!
Lord of the Hurricane! bid all thy winds
Swell, and destruction ride upon the surge,
Where, after the red lightning flash that shows
The labouring ship, all is at once deep night
And long suspense, till the slow dawn of day
Gleams on the scattered corses of the dead,
That strew the sounding shore!

Then think of him,
Ye who rejoice with those you love, at eve,
When winds of winter shake the window-frame,
And more endear your fire, oh, think of him,
Who, saved alone from the destroying storm,
Is cast on some deserted rock; who sees

Sun after sun descend, and hopeless hears;
At morn the long surge of the troubled main,
That beats without his wretched cave; meantime
He fears to wake the echoes with his voice,
So dread the solitude!

Let Greenland's snows
Then shine, and mark the melancholy train
There left to perish, whilst the cold pale day
Declines along the further ice, that binds
The ship, and leaves in night the sinking scene.
Sad winter closes on the deep; the smoke
Of frost, that late amusive to the eye
Rose o'er the coast, is passed, and all is now
One torpid blank; the freezing particles
Blown blistering, and the white bear seeks her cave.
Ill-fated outcasts, when the morn again
Shall streak with feeble beam the frozen waste,
Your air-bleached and unburied carcases
Shall press the ground, and, as the stars fade off,
Your stony eyes glare 'mid the desert snows!

These triumphs boast, fell Demon of the Deep!
Though never more the universal shriek
Of all that perish thou shalt hear, as when
The deep foundations of the guilty earth
Were shaken at the voice of God, and man
Ceased in his habitations; yet the sea
Thy might tempestuous still, and joyless rule,
Confesses. Ah! what bloodless shadows throng
Ev'n now, slow rising from their oozy beds,
From Mete, and those gates of burial
That guard the Erythræan; from the vast
Unfathomed caverns of the Western main
Or stormy Orcades; whilst the sad shell
Of poor Arion, to the hollow blast
Slow seems to pour its melancholy tones,
And faintly vibrate, as the dead pass by.

I see the chiefs, who fell in distant lands,
The prey of murderous savages, when yells,
And shouts, and conch, resounded through the woods.
Magellan and De Solis seem to lead
The mournful train. Shade of Perouse! oh, say
Where, in the tract of unknown seas, thy bones
Th' insulting surge has swept?

But who is he,

Whose look, though pale and bloody, wears the trace
Of pure philanthropy? The pitying sigh
Forbid not; he was dear to Britons, dear
To every beating heart, far as the world
Extends; and my faint faltering touch ev'n now
Dies on the strings, when I pronounce thy name,
Oh, lost, lamented, generous, hapless Cook!

But cease the vain complaint; turn from the shores,
Wet with his blood, Remembrance: cast thine eyes
Upon the long seas, and the wider world,
Displayed from his research. Smile, glowing Health!
For now no more the wasted seaman sinks,
With haggard eye and feeble frame diseased;
No more with tortured longings for the sight
Of fields and hillocks green, madly he calls
On Nature, when before his swimming eye
The liquid long expanse of cheerless seas
Seems all one flowery plain. Then frantic dreams
Arise; his eye's distemper'd flash is seen
From the sunk socket, as a demon there
Sat mocking, till he plunges in the flood,
And the dark wave goes o'er him.

Nor wilt thou,
O Science! fail to deck the cold morai
Of him who wider o'er earth's hemisphere
Thy views extended. On, from deep to deep,
Thou shalt retrace the windings of his track;
From the high North to where the field-ice binds
The still Antarctic. Thence, from isle to isle,
Thou shalt pursue his progress; and explore
New-Holland's eastern shores, where now the sons
Of distant Britain, from her lap cast out,
Water the ground with tears of penitence,
Perhaps, hereafter, in their destined time,
Themselves to rise pre-eminent. Now speed,
By Asia's eastern bounds, still to the North,
Where the vast continents of either world
Approach: Beyond, 'tis silent boundless ice,
Impenetrable barrier, where all thought
Is lost; where never yet the eagle flew,
Nor roamed so far the white bear through the waste.

But thou, dread POWER! whose voice from chaos called
The earth, who bad'st the Lord of light go forth,
Ev'n as a giant, and the sounding seas
Roll at thy fiat: may the dark deep clouds,

That thy pavilion shroud from mortal sight,
So pass away, as now the mystery,
Obscure through rolling ages, is disclosed;
How man, from one great Father sprung, his race
Spread to that severed continent! Ev'n so,
FATHER, in thy good time, shall all things stand
Revealed to knowledge.

As the mind revolves
The change of mighty empires, and the fate
Of HIM whom Thou hast made, back through the dusk
Of ages Contemplation turns her view:
We mark, as from its infancy, the world
Peopled again, from that mysterious shrine
That rested on the top of Ararat,
Highest of Asian mountains; spreading on,
The Cushites from their mountain caves descend;
Then before GOD the sons of Ammon stood
In their gigantic might, and first the seas
Vanquished: But still from clime to clime the groan
Of sacrifice, and Superstition's cry,
Was heard; but when the Dayspring rose of heaven,
Greece's hoar forests echoed, The great Pan
Is dead! From Egypt, and the rugged shores
Of Syrian Tyre, the gods of darkness fly;
Bel is cast down, and Nebo, horrid king,
Bows in imperial Babylon: But, ah!
Too soon, the Star of Bethlehem, whose ray
The host of heaven hailed jubilant, and sang,
Glory to God on high, and on earth peace,
With long eclipse is veiled.

Red Papacy
Usurped the meek dominion of the Lord
Of love and charity: vast as a fiend
She rose, Heaven's light was darkened with her frown,
And the earth murmured back her hymns of blood,
As the meek martyr at the burning stake
Stood, his last look uplifted to his GOD!
But she is now cast down, her empire reft.
They who in darkness walked, and in the shade
Of death, have seen a new and holy light,
As in th' umbrageous forest, through whose boughs,
Mossy and damp, for many a league, the morn
With languid beam scarce pierces, here and there
Touching some solitary trunk, the rest
Dark waving in the noxious atmosphere:
Through the thick-matted leaves the serpent winds

His way, to find a spot of casual sun;
The gaunt hyæna through the thicket glides
At eve: then, too, the couched tiger's eye
Flames in the dusk, and oft the gnashing jaws
Of the fell crocodile are heard. At length,
By man's superior energy and toil,
The sunless brakes are cleared; the joyous morn
Shines through the opening leaves; rich culture smiles
Around; and howling to their distant wilds
The savage inmates of the wood retire.
Such is the scene of human life, till want
Bids man his strength put forth; then slowly spreads
The cultured stream of mild humanity,
And gentler virtues, and more noble aims
Employ the active mind, till beauty beams
Around, and Nature wears her richest robe,
Adorned with lovelier graces. Then the charms
Of woman, fairest of the works of Heaven,
Whom the cold savage, in his sullen pride,
Scorned as unworthy of his equal love,
With more attractive influence wins the heart
Of her protector. Then the names of sire,
Of home, of brother, and of children, grow
More sacred, more endearing; whilst the eye,
Lifted beyond this earthly scene, beholds
A Father who looks down from heaven on all!

O Britain, my loved country! dost thou rise
Most high among the nations! Do thy fleets
Ride o'er the surge of ocean, that subdued
Rolls in long sweep beneath them! Dost thou wear
Thy garb of gentler morals gracefully!
Is widest science thine, and the fair train
Of lovelier arts! While commerce throngs thy ports
With her ten thousand streamers, is the tract
Of the undeviating ploughshare white
That rips the reeking furrow, followed soon
By plenty, bidding all the scene rejoice,
Even like a cultured garden! Do the streams
That steal along thy peaceful vales, reflect
Temples, and Attic domes, and village towers!
Is beauty thine, fairest of earthly things,
Woman; and doth she gain that liberal love
And homage, which the meekness of her voice,
The rapture of her smile, commanding most
When she seems weakest, must demand from him,
Her master; whose stern strength at once submits
In manly, but endearing, confidence,

Unlike his selfish tyranny who sits
The sultan of his harem!

Oh, then, think
How great the blessing, and how high thy rank
Amid the civilised and social world!
But hast thou no deep failings, that may turn
Thy thoughts within thyself! Ask, for the sun
That shines in heaven hath seen it, hath thy power
Ne'er scattered sorrow over distant lands!
Ask of the East, have never thy proud sails
Borne plunder from dismembered provinces,
Leaving the groans of miserable men
Behind! And free thyself, and lifting high
The charter of thy freedom, bought with blood,
Hast thou not stood, in patient apathy,
A witness of the tortures and the chains
That Afric's injured sons have known! Stand up;
Yes, thou hast visited the caves, and cheered
The gloomy haunts of sorrow; thou hast shed
A beam of comfort and of righteousness
On isles remote; hast bid the bread-fruit shade
Th' Hesperian regions, and has softened much
With bland amelioration, and with charms
Of social sweetness, the hard lot of man.
But weighed in truth's firm balance, ask, if all
Be even. Do not crimes of ranker growth
Batten amid thy cities, whose loud din,
From flashing and contending cars, ascends,
Till morn! Enchanting, as if aught so sweet
Ne'er faded, do thy daughters wear the weeds
Of calm domestic peace and wedded love;
Or turn, with beautiful disdain, to dash
Gay pleasure's poisoned chalice from their lips
Untasted! Hath not sullen atheism,
Weaving gay flowers of poesy, so sought
To hide the darkness of his withered brow
With faded and fantastic gallantry
Of roses, thus to win the thoughtless smile
Of youthful ignorance! Hast thou with awe
Looked up to Him whose power is in the clouds,
Who bids the storm rush, and it sweeps to earth
The nations that offend, and they are gone,
Like Tyre and Babylon! Well weigh thyself:
Then shalt thou rise undaunted in the might
Of thy Protector, and the gathered hate
Of hostile bands shall be but as the sand
Blown on the everlasting pyramid.

Hasten, O Love and Charity! your work,
Ev'n now whilst it is day; far as the world
Extends may your divinest influence
Be felt, and more than felt, to teach mankind
They all are brothers, and to drown the cries
Of superstition, anarchy, or blood!
Not yet the hour is come: on Ganges' banks
Still superstition hails the flame of death,
Behold, gay dressed, as in her bridal tire,
The self-devoted beauteous victim slow
Ascend the pile where her dead husband lies:
She kisses his cold cheeks, inclines her breast
On his, and lights herself the fatal pile
That shall consume them both!

On Egypt's shore,
Where Science rose, now Sloth and Ignorance
Sleep like the huge Behemoth in the sun!
The turbaned Moor still stains with strangers' blood
The inmost sands of Afric. But all these
The light shall visit, and that vaster tract
From Fuego to the furthest Labrador,
Where roam the outcast Esquimaux, shall hear
The voice of social fellowship; the chief
Whose hatchet flashed amid the forest gloom,
Who to his infants bore the bleeding scalp
Of his fall'n foe, shall weep unwonted tears!

Come, Faith; come, Hope; come, meek-eyed Charity!
Complete the lovely prospect: every land
Shall lift up one hosannah; every tongue
Proclaim thee FATHER, INFINITE, and WISE,
And GOOD. The shores of palmy Senegal
(Sad Afric's injured sons no more enslaved)
Shall answer HALLELUJAH, for the LORD
Of truth and mercy reigns;—reigns KING OF KINGS;—
HOSANNAH—KING OF KINGS—and LORD OF LORDS!

So may His kingdom come, when all the earth,
Uniting thus as in one hymn of praise,
Shall wait the end of all things. This great globe,
His awful plan accomplished, then shall sink
In flames, whilst through the clouds, that wrap the place
Where it had rolled, and the sun shone, the voice
Of the ARCHANGEL, and the TRUMP OF GOD,
Amid heaven's darkness rolling fast away,
Shall sound!

Then shall the sea give up its dead;—
But man's immortal mind, all trials past
That shook his feverish frame, amidst the scenes
Of peril and distemper, shall ascend
Exulting to its destined seat of rest,
And "justify His ways" from whom it sprung.

NOTES

Mete, in the Arabic, according to Bruce, signifies "the place of burial." The entrance of the Red Sea was so called, from the dangers of the navigation. See Bruce.

Alluding to the pathetic poem of the Shipwreck, whose author, Falconer, described himself under the name of Arion, and who was afterwards lost in the "Aurora."

"Morai" is a grave.

Botany Bay.

William Lisle Bowles – A Short Biography

William Lisle Bowles was born on 24th September 1762 at King's Sutton in Northamptonshire.

His great-grandfather, grandfather and his father, William Thomas Bowles, had all been parish priests and inevitably Bowles would join their line.

At the age of 14 he entered Winchester College, where the headmaster was Dr Joseph Warton (a minor poet, his most notable piece is The Enthusiast, 1744. In 1755, he taught at Winchester and from 1766 to 1793 was headmaster. His career as a critic was illustrious. He produced editions of poets such as Virgil as well as several English poets).

In 1789 Bowles published, a small quarto volume, Fourteen Sonnets, which was received with extraordinary praise, not only by the general public, but by such revered poets as Samuel Taylor Coleridge and Wordsworth.

The Sonnets were a return to an older and purer poetic style, and by their grace of expression, lyrical versification, tender tone of feeling and vivid appreciation of the wonder and beauty of nature, stood out in marked contrast to the elaborate works which then formed the bulk of English poetry.

Bowles said "Poetic trifles from solitary rambles whilst chewing the cud of sweet and bitter fancy, written from memory, confined to fourteen lines, this seemed best adapted to the unity of sentiment, the verse flowed in unpremeditated harmony as my ear directed but are far from being mere elegiac couplets".

The young Samuel Taylor Coleridge felt obliged to record his debt of gratitude to Bowles: "My obligations to Mr. Bowles were indeed important, and for radical good. At a very premature age, ... I had bewildered myself in metaphysicks, and in theological controversy. Nothing else pleased me. Poetry ... became insipid to me.... This preposterous pursuit was, beyond doubt, injurious both to my natural powers, and to the progress of my education.... But from this I was auspiciously withdrawn, chiefly by the genial influence of a style of poetry, so tender and yet so manly, so natural and real, and yet so dignified and harmonious, as the sonnets &c. of Mr. Bowles!"

In 1781 Bowles left as captain of Winchester school, and proceeded to Trinity College, Oxford, after winning a scholarship. Two years later he won the Chancellor's prize for Latin verse. It was now evident that the Church and poetry were to be his two callings.

After receiving his degree at Oxford, Bowles now began his career in service to the Church of England. In 1792, after serving as curate in Donhead St Andrew, Bowles was appointed vicar of Chicklade in Wiltshire.

Five years later, in 1797, he received the vicarage of Dumbleton in Gloucestershire, and in 1804 became vicar of Bremhill in Wiltshire, where he wrote the poem seen on Maud Heath's statue. In the same year his bishop, John Douglas, collated him to a prebendal stall in Salisbury Cathedral.

In 1818 Bowles was made chaplain to the Prince Regent, and in 1828 he was elected residentiary canon of Salisbury.

His years of service perhaps diminished both his stature as a poet and certainly the way he was viewed. For much of his career Bowles was seen as rather soft when set against his contemporaries but in the end his ability as a poet was enshrined, after a long and ferocious attack against him, by the principles he so eloquently wrote about and adhered too.

It is as well to remember that when critics suggest that compared to other poets his longer works were not to the standard that the competition achieved, that this era is perhaps without poetic equal. Set against Byron, Shelley, Keats, Wordsworth and other great luminaries of the era it is perhaps difficult to see his works in isolation for their own value.

The longer poems published by Bowles are distinguished by purity of imagination, cultured and graceful diction, and a great thoughtfulness of feeling. Among them were The Spirit of Discovery (1804), which alas was so mercilessly ridiculed by Byron; The Missionary (1813); The Grave of the Last Saxon (1822); and St John in Patmos (1833).

In 1806 he published an edition of Alexander Pope's works with notes and an essay, in which he laid down certain canons as to poetic imagery which, subject to some modification, were later accepted, but received at the time with strong opposition by admirers of Pope.

Bowles restated his views in 1819, in The Invariable Principles of Poetry. The controversy brought into sharp contrast the opposing views of poetry, which may be thought of as being either the natural or the artificial.

In personality and nature Bowles was said to be an amiable, absent-minded, but rather eccentric man. His poems speak warmly of a refinement of feeling, tenderness, and pensive thought, but are lacking in power and passion. But that should not diminish their value or appreciation to us.

Bowles maintained that images drawn from nature are poetically finer than those drawn from art; and that in the highest kinds of poetry the themes or passions handled should be of the general or elemental kind, and not the transient manners of any society. These positions were attacked by Byron, Thomas Campbell, William Roscoe and others, and for a time Bowles had to fight his corner on his own. Soon however, William Hazlitt and the Blackwood critics came to his assistance, and on the whole Bowles had reason to congratulate himself on having established certain principles which might serve as the basis of a true method of poetical criticism, and of having inaugurated, both by precept and by example, a new era in English poetry.

As well as his poetry Bowles was also responsible for writing a Life of Bishop Ken (in two volumes, 1830–1831), Coombe Ellen and St. Michael's Mount (1798), The Battle of the Nile (1799), and The Sorrows of Switzerland (1801).

Bowles also enjoyed considerable reputation as an antiquary and his principal work in that field was Hermes Britannicus (1828).

William Lisle Bowles died on April 7th, 1850 at the age of 87.

www.ingramcontent.com/pod-product-compliance
Lightning Source LLC
Chambersburg PA
CBHW060054050426

42448CB00011B/2458